The Truth About Spiritual Enlightenment

Shanmugam P

I would like to dedicate this book to these two important people who played a role in shaping me, nurturing me and tutoring me:

1) To **Mrs. Dhanalakshmi,** my Tamil teacher at Sri Kailasam Memorial High School, T.M.Puram, Tirunelveli dist, Tamil Nadu, India

2) To **Mrs. Usha Raman,** the principal of Sri Jayendra Saraswathi Swamigal Golden Jubilee Matriculation Higher Secondary School, Sankarnagar, Tirunelveli, Tamil Nadu, India

Table of Contents

Contents

Introduction

Many years ago, a 18 year old boy became frustrated with his life and decided to end his life. He had lost all his hope and he couldn't find any reason to live. He was lonely, insecure and totally dissatisfied with the way things were happening to him. But then he started to think about his decision, "The worst thing that can happen to me is my death and I am ready to die. If I have the courage to face death, why shouldn't I have the same courage to face life? Death can wait for me; I can postpone it as long as I want. If I had made up my mind to die, why should I die today? What is the hurry? I can die when it is no longer bearable. I can just live my life whichever way I want; and if it gets too much, then I will choose death".

The young guy didn't die. He decided to wait. He lived, learned, contemplated on life, meditated now and then and went through a rigorous spiritual journey. About a decade later, he grew up to be a peaceful, happy and fulfilled man with no signs of depression, anxiety or misery. He is the author of this book. Yeah, thats me!

This book is a detailed account of everything that I learnt, experienced and realized in my life. After analysing Buddhist and Vedantic scriptures in the light of my own experience, I put together a detailed guide for subjective well being, peace and fulfillment that everyone is searching for in their life. It is not based on faith but it is an empirical approach to a peaceful and happy life. This book is a sincere attempt to bridge Science, Buddhism and Advaita Vedanta. So, this is not about blind beliefs, unexplained rituals, complicated dogmas or boring theories. This book gives you an empirical method to attain ultimate fulfillment, peace and happiness.

India is home for six orthodox philosophical schools of thought as well as a few heterodox schools. This land was home to many wise men and sages. For the last 3500 years, so much things have been written about human suffering and cessation of suffering. Many schools seem to have teachings which are contradictory to other schools. Buddha says one thing; Shankara says another thing; Science says something totally different. How do we reconcile all this? That is what I have done in this book. I am going to show you how Buddhism, Vedanta and Science are saying essentially the same thing.

Make sure you read all the chapters in the same order. Take your time in reading and understanding each chapter before you move on to the next chapter.

- Shanmugam P

Chapter One: Are We Really Happy?

"How are you" is probably one of the most asked questions in everyday conversations. When you meet a person after a long time, your first question to him is regarding his subjective well being. This obviously indicates a fact: Your subjective well being is the most important thing in your life. Everyone strives for a happy, satisfied and peaceful life. It is the only reason why people want to make more money, become more successful or work day and night. Even if you want to sacrifice the pleasures of your life for a good cause, it is still based on the fact that you feel good about it.

But this search for the happiness never stops. You have to keep striving for maintaining a certain level of happiness in your life. When I was a child, I thought that becoming a grown up is all I have to do to be permanently peaceful and happy. But once you are grown up, you know that there are thousands of things which can cause you stress. Stress and depression is a very common problem for a lot of people in life. Above all, there is always an underlying dissatisfaction in life with the way things are. We always want certain things to be different to make us happy. This search for happiness and making efforts for our well-being continues throughout our lives even though the level of happiness is always the same. We have hopes and dreams for future which seem to be promising ultimate well being. Most of the people go through their lives with dreams about the future and a hope that they will be more happier in the future than how they are today.

This is not to say that we don't enjoy our lives. We do. But this enjoyment needs constant protection and also gives you a feeling that this is not enough. You want more. You are not satisfied yet. While you are in the pursuit of searching for more money, more experience and more knowledge in life, your existing level of happiness can also be threatened by any number of things that can happen in your life. Fear and anxiety seems to be always a part of life and a life without worries seems to be impossible.

Psychologists say that people have a stable level of happiness that we maintain throughout our lives. Any negative or positive things that happen in our lives may decrease or increase the level of happiness temporarily but we always tend to return to this stable level of happiness. No matter how much money you make or how popular you become, there is not going to be a permanent gain in the level of happiness. But this level of happiness that we maintain is not something that gives us 100% satisfaction. So, we tend to do things to increase this level but return to the same old baseline happiness level again and again. Psychologists call this as hedonic treadmill.

Hedonic Treadmill

'Hedonic treadmill' is a term coined by psychologists Brickman and Campbell during 1971 in their essay titled 'Hedonic Relativism and Planning the Good Society'. More than a decade later, Michael

William Eysenck, a British academic psychologist, developed a psychology theory known as 'hedonic treadmill theory' by modifying this concept. Philip Brickman, Dan Coates and Ronnie Janoff-Bulman did a study that examined two groups of people: A group that won a large amount of money in lottery and another group of people who got paralysed due to an accident. Based on this research, they published the paper "Lottery Winners and Accident Victims: Is Happiness Relative?" in 1987. Our logic may suggest that people who won the lottery should be more happier than the people who were paralysed. But it was found that in the long term, neither of these groups appeared happier than the other.

Many further studies were conducted in the following years that gave more clarity to this hedonic treadmill theory. But one thing is clear from the theory: there seems to be no correlation between happiness and objective outcomes in the long term. The metaphor of hedonic treadmill indicates that in spite of the efforts that we make to increase the happiness, human happiness always seems to remain stationary. But if no efforts are made, happiness seems to decline. This makes us to constantly run on the hedonic treadmill for our entire lives.

There is another metaphor which can be applied to this. A human being lives his life as if his mind constantly on fire. Our fears, anxiety, hatred, delusion and dissatisfaction can be likened to fires that are burning incessantly.

Unsatisfactoriness and Suffering in Life

So, let us first understand this as an important truth: There is an underlying dissatisfaction, stress and restlessness in life which makes a person prone to suffering. Of course, this doesn't mean that people are always suffering or that the life is entirely miserable. But we can't rest in peace when we are living. 'Rest in peace' is always associated with death because our mind hardly finds any rest. We have a big to-do list and agenda for our future. As long as the to-do list is ok, life seems to go on. But if something goes wrong in the to-do list or if our hopes and dreams are threatened, we suffer.

This truth is the first of the four noble truths given by Gautama Buddha about 2600 years ago. This first noble truth addresses the underlying dissatisfaction and stress in life. According to this noble truth, a human being is prone to sorrow, lamentation, pain, distress and despair. He feels miserable when he doesn't get what he wants, in the association of unpleasant and separation from the pleasant and because of the feeling that things never measure up to his expectations or standards.

Is it possible to liberate ourselves from this trap of hedonic treadmill or should we keep running on it our entire life? Is it possible to burn out the fires which are constantly burning or there is no choice? Many of the ancient traditions originated from India say that it is indeed possible to get liberated from the trap of this hedonic treadmill. They promise us that this incessantly burning fires of hatred, delusion and greed can be burnt out. There are two popular words which are synonymous to the liberation from the trap that we are talking about: Moksha and Nirvana.

The word Moksha literally means liberation. It comes from the Sanskrit root 'much' (the 'u' is pronounced as it is pronounced in the English word 'full'). This root word means to free, release, to let go or to liberate. Nirvana, mostly used in Buddhist context, means 'blown out' or 'extinguished'. The word is used to indicate that the incessant fires of greed, hatred, delusion etc are blown out. Liberation gives the ultimate fulfillment and peace.

The Cause of Suffering

The word 'suffering' can mean many things to many people. But in this book, I am going to use the word 'suffering' to indicate all the points that we discussed just now when explaining the first noble truth. What is the cause of this suffering? Buddha explained it in the second noble truth.

This suffering is caused by craving. We crave for three things: Craving for pleasure, craving for becoming and craving for non-becoming. Note that Buddha is not giving a moral code here, he is simply stating a fact. It doesn't mean that you should suppress your desires; Instead, throughout this book, we are going to discuss the actual and systematic way to end your craving without having to either suppress them or to mindlessly give in to the temptations of your desires.

Let me first explain these three kinds of craving. We all know what craving for pleasure is. Craving for becoming is nothing but wanting to become as somebody. You may want to become rich, knowledgeable or famous. It is not that becoming rich or famous is wrong. We are not discussing what is wrong or what is right. We are just discussing the root cause of the underlying dissatisfaction. If you want to become famous, then you already know that you are not going to be satisfied unless it happens. But even when it happens, you will still strive to become even more famous. Thus, you will be stuck in the treadmill forever. The third type of craving is craving for nonexistence. If you want to kill yourself and disappear, that is also a form of craving. When you want to annihilate yourself, it essentially means that you don't want to face the unpleasant experiences in your life.

There is one thing we need to understand here. Before the final liberation, craving is natural and it is prone to continue. If you deliberately seek or intent to end your craving, that is another form of craving anyway. But instead of suppressing your craving, you are going to bring in more awareness to your mental processes, observe and understand your mind and let craving lose its energy gradually. As you understand more and more about the path to liberation, your craving for multiple things in the world may naturally get focused as an intense desire for liberation itself. When your whole energy is invested towards the spiritual path, the progress will be quite natural. In fact, desire for liberation is a desired prerequisite to walk on the spiritual path. For example Vedanta calls the desire for liberation as 'Mumukshutva' and lists it as one of the prerequisites for spiritual practice.

Cessation of Suffering and the Path

The third and fourth noble truth in Buddhism is just this. The third truth conveys that cessation of suffering is possible. In the fourth truth, Buddha talks about the noble way to end suffering, the noble eightfold path.

However, the path I am going to discuss in this book is not an exact replica of this noble eightfold path. In this book, I am going to combine the concepts from both Buddhism and Vedanta, back up with the concepts of psychology wherever it is necessary and guide you to find your own way. There is no need to run away from life or renounce the world. There is no need to surrender to someone, volunteer for an organization, become a member of cult or even spend time in hours and hours of sitting meditation. Sitting meditations can help and will be also described in this book but more emphasis and importance will be on how to turn your everyday activities into spiritual practice.

The practice can be integrated into everything that you do in your daily life. In other words, your actual life can be turned to a powerful spiritual practice. Above all, there is no need to believe in anything. There isn't going to be anything paranormal, supernatural or magical that you have to believe in. All this is based on my own experience.

The solution for the liberation is simple but it is not easy. This is not like a get rich quick scheme or a quick path to fast food enlightenment. It requires awareness and extreme courage to walk on this path. However, it is necessary to focus on the journey rather than the destination. The whole idea is to make the journey more important, juicy, interesting and thrilling without worrying too much about the destination. As you keep reading the book, you will also realize a striking paradox, that there is actually no journey and there is no person who is making the journey in the first place. If you don't understand this yet, don't worry; just keep reading!

Chapter Two: Basic Theory: The Subject and the Object

Before we move on, you have to learn to make an important discrimination: subject vs object. This discrimination is very important. If you can understand the concept behind discrimination between these two, then your spiritual journey will be a lot easier.

I am using the terms 'subject' and 'object' only as a convenience, to explain the basics. So, I will just define these two words to let you know what exactly I mean by them. You may not find these meanings in any dictionary. These words are just used for the sake of explanation. I could have used other words, but sometimes those words cause unnecessary confusion. I will tell you why in a moment.

So, let me first get the terminology straight.

The 'object' is anything that is observable through our five senses and through our own mental awareness. So, it is not limited to the external objects that you see, smell, hear, touch or taste but also applies to all the internal objects such as thoughts, feelings, sensations etc. In other words, anything that you can observe or notice in anyway is an object.

Normally, the thoughts and feelings are defined as subjective. Cambridge dictionary defines the word 'Subjective' as 'influenced by or based on personal beliefs or feelings, rather than based on facts'. But you can also notice your own thoughts and feelings. You can approach your own mind with an attitude of objectivity. The contents of consciousness can be carefully noticed by you at any moment, as if they have got nothing to do with you.

Is it possible to step back from the train of your thought stream and notice it as if you are an outsider? Yes it is possible. So, what is this 'you' which is actually noticing the thoughts? It is the pure subject that is devoid of any attributes. Because, any attribute will come under the category of an object. So, the important thing that you need to understand about the subject is, it is not an object at all. The subject cannot be noticed because it is the one which actually notices. This doesn't mean that the subject is actually a hidden entity inside our head. By understanding this way, you are again making the 'subject' into an object. This pure subject cannot be conceptualized in anyway. It is like a witness that observes both the body and the mental processes.

Discrimination between these two is like an art or knack that you have to learn. You may misunderstand in the beginning and mistake an object of your consciousness as the subject. This tends to happen so often. But whenever you recognize it when it happens, you will become more smart and skillful in this discrimination. If you just try to witness your thought process, sensations, your emotions, your body movements etc as a passive, curious, non-judgemental observer every moment, the distinction between subject and the objects will become more and more obvious. If you can try to maintain this constant stream of passive, non-judgemental awareness even for 10 minutes, a new door will open up for the endless observation of your mind. I will describe more about this practice in the upcoming chapters. But for now, just remember this: The ability to discriminate between the subject and the object, the observer and the observed, is very important and crucial. You may want to read this chapter again and again until you get a firm understanding of this.

It is important to realize that this subject is unchanging. But everything else in your consciousness keeps changing. It can be compared to the moving pictures in a movie screen. The pictures change constantly but the screen remains the same. When we are engrossed in the movie, we completely forget about the screen. The same thing happens when we think. We are completely engrossed and identified with our thoughts that we never step back from those thoughts to actually observe them.

The Observer Self - Acceptance and Commitment therapy

In psychology and psychotherapy, this 'subject' is called with many names such 'observer self', 'self as observer', 'self as context' or 'perspective taking'. This concept is widely used in Acceptance and

Commitment therapy, a form of cognitive-behavior therapy. Dr. Russ Harris, a psychotherapist and world-renowned trainer of Acceptance & Commitment Therapy defines observer self as follows, in his book 'ACT made simple':

> "In everyday language, we talk about the "mind" without recognizing that there are two distinct elements to it: the thinking self and the observing self. We're all very familiar with the thinking self: that part of us which is always thinking—generating thoughts, beliefs, memories, judgments, fantasies, plans, and so on. But most people are unfamiliar with the observing self: the aspect of us that is aware of whatever we're thinking, feeling, sensing, or doing in any moment. Another term for it is "pure awareness." In ACT, the technical term is self-as-context. For example, as you go through life, your body changes, your thoughts change, your feelings change, your roles change, but the "you" that's able to notice or observe all those things never changes. It's the same "you" that's been there your whole life. With clients, we generally refer to it as "the observing self" rather than use the technical term "self-as-context."

While they define the subject as 'Observer self', the self that is observed by it is called as 'conceptualized self'. Conceptualized self is the image of the self that you carry in your head, the self-concept, which contains stories, descriptions, opinions, hopes, dreams etc. It is an object of consciousness which can be noticed by the observer-self.

Steven C. Hayes, Department of Psychology, University of Nevada, says the following in his article 'Acceptance and Commitment Therapy as a Unified Model of Behavior Change':

> *"When people are asked about themselves, they tend to describe the conceptualized self—their self-narrative (e.g., "I am someone who always tries hard"). The conceptualized self often reduces behavioral flexibility because the attempt to be right about such descriptions can lead to rejection of contradictory content. Events that threaten the conceptualized self can evoke strong emotions and lead to heightened experiential avoidance based on the need for consistency within the narrative (Mendolia & Baker, 2008). When a person overidentifies with a particular self-conceptualization, events outside the narrative can seem to invalidate life itself, as illustrated by a string of recent suicides of extremely wealthy individuals who have lost their fortunes in the international economic downturn. Directly changing self-concepts can be difficult (e.g., Baumeister, Campbell, Krueger, & Vohs, 2003), but an alternative is provided by a transcendent, noticing sense of self. Because of relational frames such as "I vs. You," "Now vs. Then," and "Here vs. There" (termed in RFT deictic relations), human language leads to a sense of self as a locus or perspective. Conscious experience develops an "I / here / now" quality that integrates into a sense of a "noticing self" (Rehfeldt, Dillen, Ziomek, & Kowalchuk, 2007). The emergence of*

this sense of self is important in ACT for two reasons. First, we now know that the same cognitive processes that give rise to it also lead to understanding the perspective of others (McHugh, Barnes-Holmes, & Barnes-Holmes, 2004), caring about others (Villatte, Monestès, McHugh, Freixa i Baqué, & Loas, 2008), and thus functioning socially (Brune, 2005). Second, a noticing self provides a secure psychological space for facing painful emotions or thoughts (Hayes, 1984). In ACT, contact with this sense of self is fostered by mindfulness exercises, metaphors, and perspective-taking experiential processes."

- *From 'Acceptance and Commitment Therapy as a Unified Model of Behavior Change' by Steven C. Hayes, Jacqueline Pistorello and Michael E. Levin*

Both Acceptance and commitment therapy and spiritual traditions agree with a basic fact even though it is expressed in different ways. When Buddha says life is suffering he actually says that our current psychological processes which motivate craving, delusion, attachment and aversion cause suffering. Hence, they are not normal even though they are universally considered as normal. ACT uses the word 'Destructive normality' as a definition for this phenomena. One of the assumptions of ACT is that the psychological processes of a normal human mind are often destructive, and create psychological suffering for us all, sooner or later (Harris, Russ, 1938).

Dr. Russ Harris says the following in his book 'ACT made simple' :

"Furthermore, ACT postulates that the root of this suffering is human language itself. Human language is a highly complex system of symbols, which includes words, images, sounds, facial expressions and physical gestures. We use this language in two domains: public and private. The public use of language includes speaking, talking, miming, gesturing, writing, painting, singing, dancing and so on. The private use of language includes thinking, imagining, daydreaming, planning, visualising and so on. A more technical term for the private use of language is 'cognition'. "

Dr. Russ Harris explains the six core principles of ACT in his book. Out of those, the first four principles have to be remembered in the spiritual path as well. Here is the excerpt from the first chapter of his book which explains those first four core principles. You have to remember these core principles throughout your spiritual journey. Since he has worded it quite well, I am including the exact text without any modification:

"Contacting the Present Moment (Be Here Now)

Contacting the present moment means being psychologically present: consciously connecting with and engaging in whatever is happening in this moment. Humans find it very hard to stay present. Like other humans, we know how easy it is to get caught up in our thoughts and lose touch with the world around us. We may spend a lot of time

absorbed in thoughts about the past or the future.
Or instead of being fully conscious of our
experience, we may operate on automatic pilot,
merely "going through the motions." Contacting the
present moment means flexibly bringing our
awareness to either the physical world around us or
the psychological world within us, or to both
simultaneously.

It also means consciously paying attention to our
here-and-now experience instead of drifting off into
our thoughts or operating on "automatic pilot."

Defusion (Watch Your Thinking)

Defusion means learning to "step back" and separate
or detach from our thoughts, images, and memories.
(The full term is "cognitive defusion," but usually we
just call it "defusion.") Instead of getting caught up
in our thoughts or being pushed around by them, we
let them come and go as if they were just cars driving
past outside our house. We step back and watch our
thinking instead of getting tangled up in it. We see
our thoughts for what they are—nothing more or
less than words or pictures. We hold them lightly
instead of clutching them tightly.

Acceptance (Open Up)

Acceptance means opening up and making room for painful feelings, sensations, urges, and emotions. We drop the struggle with them, give them some breathing space, and allow them to be as they are. Instead of fighting them, resisting them, running from them, or getting overwhelmed by them, we open up to them and let them be. (Note: This doesn't mean liking them or wanting them. It simply means making room for them!)

Self-as-Context (Pure Awareness)

In everyday language, we talk about the "mind" without recognizing that there are two distinct elements to it: the thinking self and the observing self. We're all very familiar with the thinking self: that part of us which is always thinking—generating thoughts, beliefs, memories, judgments, fantasies, plans, and so on. But most people are unfamiliar with the observing self: the aspect of us that is aware of whatever we're thinking, feeling, sensing, or doing in any moment. Another term for it is "pure awareness." In ACT, the technical term is self-as-context. For example, as you go through life, your body changes, your thoughts change, your feelings change, your roles change, but the "you" that's able to notice or observe all those things never changes. It's the same "you" that's been there your whole life.

> *With clients, we generally refer to it as "the*
> *observing self" rather than use the technical term*
> *"self-as-context."*
>
> - *Harris, Russ, 1938 - ACT made simple*

While Acceptance and commitment therapy is just a clinical therapy used to treat anxiety disorders, depression and addiction, the methods used in this therapy are very useful when you are learning how to discriminate between the subject and the object and how to witness the contents of your consciousness.

Vedanta - Self vs self

Vedanta says that this 'subject' is the actual 'You'. It says that you are not your thoughts, you are not your body, you are not your emotions and you are not your mind.

Here, we need to remember that 'You' or 'I' is just words. In everyday conversation, we just use the words 'You' and 'I' as points of reference. But when you say 'I', it obviously refers to something which is more important for you, the person which is you, that includes your body and your mind. When Vedanta says you are not your mind or body, it doesn't give you a new meaning to the word 'I', but it is actually a device to help you develop this 'observer self'.

Because, only when you assume the subject as you and only when you take the side of a witness, you can pay attention to the thought process and your body, without getting identified with them. Even in the Acceptance & Commitment therapy, they use a questionnaire to ask various questions to make the clients switch the side from the conceptualized self to the observer self. They also use various metaphors to make them understand. Because, even though the concept is very simple, understanding it may be still very difficult.

Taking such terminology so seriously has opened room for a lot of unnecessary debates and arguments. I recently watched a debate between a spiritual leader and a skeptic. The spiritual leader said 'What you call as your body and your mind is only an accumulation. You are not your body. You are not your mind either'. The skeptic replied, "This is absolute nonsense... This is like saying that you have to keep peeling the layers of onion until you find the onion. The layers are the onion. The mind and body is you. There is no you apart from the mind and the body."

Such arguments will be never ending. Because, both of them are actually arguing over the meaning of the word 'I'. The spiritual leader defines the word 'I' as the subject, the observer self which is not an entity. The skeptic interprets that as some kind of philosophy and thinks that the spiritual leader is talking about some kind of entity that exists apart from body and mind.

But his onion example also has a spiritual significance. Actually, when you go through the spiritual practice for long term, you will actually feel like peeling the layers of your mind to inquire who you are.. As days go by, you will feel like a lot of layers of mind are actually getting peeled. You will naturally be curious and longing to find out what will happen when all the layers all peeled.If you can't understand this metaphor now, don't worry. You will eventually understand it as you progress in your journey.

After liberation, the experience of reality doesn't have the division of 'me vs world'. All the distinctions and mental boundaries between you and the world disappears. There is no feeling that there is an 'other'. This experience of oneness is usually called as non-duality in modern times. When the experience of reality is nondual 24/7, words like 'I' and 'You' have meaning only in communication. Other than that the 'I' doesn't really have much importance. Because the word 'I' always implies that there is an other. Even the statement 'I am truth, consciousness and bliss' implies duality. This is the problem when we try to put non-duality in words, because the language itself is a product of duality.

So, it is very important to make this clear again, so that you don't get confused. The subject or the observer self is not an entity or an object that can be observed in anyway. Also, when someone says 'You are not your body and you are not your mind', it is not a philosophy but a method. He or she is actually teaching you to take the place of the subject, instead of getting identified with the objects or the contents of your consciousness. This subject is self evident. It is like an internal light which makes the contents of the consciousness noticeable.

Some of the modern teachers of Vedanta distinguish between the 'I' as a person and the 'I' as the subject using the words 'self' and 'Self' (with a capital S) respectively. Here, you need to notice that the person that you call as 'I', the self, is actually an image in your head, which is also an object that can be witnessed by the subject. You have a self-image, don't you?

Let me define it in a different way so that you understand this very clearly. We all have concepts about various things in this world. The concepts are fundamental building blocks of our thoughts. When we were young, we acquired concepts about various things in the world. A concept is a mental representation that represents an external object. We also have concepts about our internal objects as well. Psychology uses the word 'mental representation' when it talks about concepts. People have a huge web of interlinked concepts in their minds, which has become so complicated and solidified over the years. Among all these concepts, there is a specific concept called 'self-concept' which is nothing but the collection of all the beliefs, thoughts and concepts about yourself. So, the mental representation in your head about the person called 'You' is actually this self-concept. This self-concept itself is made up of thoughts and beliefs, which can be observed by the subject. We will talk more about this self-concept in the next chapter.

Vedanta and Samkhya on subject-object discrimination

The oldest traditions of India call the subject as Purusha and the object as Prakriti. They are usually translated as consciousness and matter. But it is very important to realize that even the thoughts and emotions belong to the category of 'object'. So, the word 'matter' can be little misleading. This discrimination of purusha and prakriti was first used by the Samkhya school of thought, which was adopted by other schools like yoga.

Vedanta uses the words 'Brahman and 'Maya' for the same. Brahman is the pure witness (the subject) which doesn't change whereas everything that is witnessed by Brahman constantly changes. Vedanta says Brahman is real and Maya is unreal. When it says unreal, it doesn't mean it doesn't exist. It means that Maya is constantly changing. So, Vedanta calls that which doesn't change as real. In other words, according to Vedanta, the definition of reality is that which doesn't change.

Let us also try to understand another key concept of Vedanta. Vedanta says that this 'subject' or Brahman is everything. It says that everything in the world is Brahman. Just as different vessels of clay is made up of the same substance, everything that you see in the world are modifications of Brahman. This is not a fact about the objective world but it is often misunderstood that way. You are never going to find Brahman by dissecting the matter or inspecting an atom. What Vedanta is talking about is the mental representation of all these objects in our consciousness.

If you really think about this, you can understand that everything is actually happening within you. Again, don't misunderstand. I am not talking any science here. This has absolutely nothing to do with physics or chemistry. This has to do with your experience of reality.

When you see a tree, you are actually seeing the tree because of the perception that is created in your brain. Everything from the outside world is actually recreated inside you in someway. Without a conscious knower of the tree, the tree doesn't really exist. In order to even say that a tree exists, there has to be a conscious knower of the tree in the first place.

This doesn't mean that the world will cease to exist after your death. Of course it won't. But how do you know this? You know this only by inference. You see people dying everyday and the world didn't disappear after their death. But in order to infer all this, there must be a consciousness in the first place, right? It seems like you are the basis of existence. You should be there in the first place to know or say that the world exists.

And, everything in the world is actually known to you through these mental representations and mental images which you witness in your mind. You have a concept about everything in your mind. Many of those concepts were acquired when you were too young. But it is consciousness that actually shines all these mental objects like concepts, thoughts and memories. All these mental objects are actually like the modifications of consciousness itself. It is in this sense that it was said that everything is Brahman.

But there is a main difference between Vedanta and Samkhya. Vedanta says that Brahman is one but Samkhya says that there are multiple purushas. Both seem to be contradictory but they are looking at things from different perspectives. When Vedanta says that there is one consciousness, it actually doesn't talk anything about the external world. It only talks about your inner world. Even though you see multiple conscious beings, what you see is actually seen in your consciousness. It is you as the subject which notices all this multiplicity. As I already explained, it talks about the one thing that never changes, which is the subject. But when Samkhya says that there are multiple purushas, it takes all the human beings with their own individual conscious fields into account. When you see another human being, you understand by inference that there is a different field of consciousness that is totally private to that person. By going by the inference, there should actually be multiple subjects in the world. In other words, Vedantic theory was proposed according to the experience whereas the theory of Samkhya was created according to the inference.

It is because of these theories that people sometimes get confused. To add to this confusion, there has been creation theories proposed in upanishads and many other ancient texts. Vedantic theory argues that the world was created from consciousness; Samkhya argues that world was created from the unconscious principle or Prakriti. It is important to understand that these metaphysical theories were created thousands of years ago when many things about the universe were not known.

This has been a problem for many centuries which caused a lot of people to believe that all these schools are talking about the reality of the physical world. But neither spirituality nor science knows the exact relationship between consciousness and matter yet.

The origin of the universe or the truth about the material world are immaterial to end our suffering. It may feed the curiosity of people who wonder about these things but it doesn't really have any place in the journey towards ending your own suffering. Wondering whether world came from consciousness or matter is a question that we have to leave to the scientists. You don't have to know the answer to this question to liberate yourself from suffering.

Among everyone who provided proper guidance for liberation, Gautama Buddha was very important. He didn't encourage any system that required blind beliefs and he always discouraged philosophical questions. Buddha was usually silent when people asked him metaphysical questions. He won't answer if anyone asks 'What is the source of existence, why am i here"

There is a beautiful parable called 'Parable of the poisoned arrow' which is about what Buddha said when someone asked metaphysical questions:

> "It's just as if a man were wounded with an arrow thickly smeared with poison. His friends & companions, kinsmen & relatives would provide him with a surgeon, and the man would say, 'I won't have this arrow removed until I know whether the man who wounded me was a noble warrior, a brahman, a merchant, or a worker.' He would say, 'I won't have this arrow removed until I know the given name & clan name of the man who wounded me... until I know whether he was tall, medium, or short... until I know whether he was

dark, ruddy-brown, or golden-colored... until I know his home village, town, or city... until I know whether the bow with which I was wounded was a long bow or a crossbow... until I know whether the bowstring with which I was wounded was fiber, bamboo threads, sinew, hemp, or bark... until I know whether the shaft with which I was wounded was wild or cultivated... until I know whether the feathers of the shaft with which I was wounded were those of a vulture, a stork, a hawk, a peacock, or another bird... until I know whether the shaft with which I was wounded was bound with the sinew of an ox, a water buffalo, a langur, or a monkey.' He would say, 'I won't have this arrow removed until I know whether the shaft with which I was wounded was that of a common arrow, a curved arrow, a barbed, a calf-toothed, or an oleander arrow.' The man would die and those things would still remain unknown to him.

In the same way, if anyone were to say, 'I won't live the holy life under the Blessed One as long as he does not declare to me that 'The cosmos is eternal,'... or that 'After death a Tathagata neither exists nor does not exist,' the man would die and those things would still remain undeclared by the Tathagata."

- "Cula-Malunkyovada Sutta: The Shorter Instructions to Malunkya" (MN 63), translated from the Pali by Thanissaro Bhikkhu. Access to Insight (BCBS Edition), 30 November 2013,

http://www.accesstoinsight.org/tipitaka/mn/mn.063.than.
html

The important thing to understand is, all these concepts were not originally created to convey any scientific truths about the world. They are only made as teaching devices or aids. The only thing which has to be focused on is how to make the distinction between everything that is observed and the one which observes everything. It all boils down to the discrimination of subject and object.

The clear understanding of how to distinguish between these two is considered as a necessary qualification to have before you even begin to walk on the spiritual path. This ability of discrimination is called as 'viveka' in Sanskrit.

In Vedanta, viveka, the ability to discriminate between the subject and object is considered as one of the prerequisites for walking in a spiritual path. I would say that this is the first and crucial step. So, make sure you spend your time in understanding this very clearly.

Chapter Three: The Problem with the Words

This chapter discusses certain concepts which are rarely discussed. We are going to discuss some inherent problems in language and communication. Understanding them will help you to avoid a lot of misunderstandings. Even though all these concepts are not directly related to human liberation itself, being aware of these things will help you to understand this book and other spiritual books.

Semantic discord

There is a reason why I wanted to define the words I am using, before we proceed any further. Because, terminology has caused a lot of problems in the world. Many debates and discussions are actually caused by both sides using one word to define two different things. Because of this, sometimes the whole discussion is about how to define a particular word. So, let us take a break from the actual topic we are discussing in this book and take a minute to understand this.

When two people are disagreeing with each other because of fundamental misunderstanding of the meaning of the terms used in a discussion, it is called as 'semantic discord'.

This is very important to address. You need to realize this as a primary reason for a lot of misunderstandings and confusion. In fact, the reason why many spiritual traditions are seen as contradictory to each other is because of the difference in terminology. This difference in terminology can cause further confusion when a word from one language is translated into another.

For example, let us take the word 'God'. Usually, the word God means an invisible person who created the world, rules it, answers our prayers and punishes the evildoers. But there is a word 'Brahman' in Vedanta, which is synonymous with the subject, the Self or the observer self. This is usually translated as God in English. It is also understood as God by most of the indians. If you are an atheist and if you hear someone talking about realizing or attaining God, he may be talking about getting liberated. These two different meanings for the same word has actually been existing in the Indian traditions before it was even translated to English. If you start a debate with a person regarding the existence of God, you need to at least define the meaning of the word God and come to an agreement with the person who you are debating with.

Another example is the word 'Mind'. The English word mind collectively refers to most of the functions of the brain like memory, intellect, our likes and dislikes etc. The word mind also includes consciousness. But in Indian traditions, there is a Sanskrit word called 'manas' which refers to only one part of the mind, the part of the mind which engages in likes, dislikes, hopes and desires. The word manas is usually translated as mind in English, which has caused a lot of confusion.

There is also a term called Ahankara which refers to the feeling 'I am the doer'. The term Ahankara is translated as ego which sometimes causes further confusion. Ahankara, Buddhi(intellect), chitta(memory) and manas are collectively called as anthakarana which is still not a direct synonym for the word 'mind', because anthakarana excludes consciousness.

The next example for this problem is the word soul. The English word soul means a non-physical entity that resides in the body. But the word Atman, which actually means the Self (the subject) and synonymous with the word Brahman is actually translated as soul in English. Many Indians also understand the word Atman as an entity living inside the body. But Atman is not an entity or an object; it is the subject or the observer self.

The same problem exists for the word Purusha. This word has been used to mean various things in Indian scriptures. The word Purusha means a cosmic man in Vedas. In common usage, the word Purusha always denotes a person.

Because of the assignment of different meanings to the same word or same meaning to two different words, a lot of confusion has happened in the way people in India and the world understand spirituality and spiritual traditions. So whenever you read anything about spirituality or discuss anything with people, make sure you understand what they mean by a particular word.

Connotation

Let me narrate something that happened in my own life to explain the meaning of connotation. When I was 15 years old, the movies which were released in Tamil had one central theme - Love, the romantic love between a man and a woman. All those movies used to glorify this romantic love as if it was the most important thing in life. Many dialogues in movies were about what true love was. This made me to get emotionally attached to the word 'Love'. Being in true love with a girl was considered by me as a virtue that I should have.

During those days, I had a crush on a girl. These days I can tell you definitely that what I had was just an attraction and attachment towards the girl. It was a desire. But I called it 'Love'. And I also made sure that what I think, say and do fits into the description of the word 'love'. Having my feelings recognized as true 'love' was more important. If someone said that it was not true love but merely a product of attraction to the opposite sex, admiration towards a person or a desire to posses, I would feel offended. Why? I had emotional attachment towards the word 'love', because the word has positive connotation.

The word God also has positive connotations. I have noticed a strange phenomenon. As we discussed before, the word God is commonly understood as an invisible person, who answers our prayers and punishes evil doers. If you tell a devout theist that God is not a person but an all-pervading power, all pervading love or all-pervading consciousness, he might accept it. But if you tell him that there is no God, he would deny it. He simply doesn't want you to word it that way. He can never accept that there is no God but it is ok for him if the word God is used in a different meaning. This is the result of connotation. Probably because of this reason, many people had to express spirituality in religious terminology.

The word 'Enlightenment' also has positive connotations. I see that as a corrupted word. Many people want to claim enlightenment simply because for them, being known as 'enlightened' feels good. I have seen many spiritual teachers twisting the meaning of the word 'enlightenment' so that it fits into the way they experience life and the way they behave. When travelling on the spiritual path, it is very important to let go of attachment to the words; otherwise you will end up fooling yourself.

Finger Pointing to the Moon

There is a saying in Buddhist traditions: The teachings are like finger pointing to the moon.

When someone is using his finger to point to the moon, a one year old kid would look at his finger. It cannot understand that it is supposed to look at the direction that the finger is pointing to. But as an adult you can understand what you are supposed to do. When a spiritual teacher is instructing you, you need to treat his words as finger pointing to the moon too. The reason this is mentioned is because people often get too attached to the words and concepts.

You may hear many spiritual teachers saying that words are just pointers. They use words to point out to the truth. Instead of focusing on words, you need to look at where the words are pointing to.

Chapter Four: Basic Theory - The Self Concept

In this chapter, we are going to deal with another important concept. This is again very important to understand because one thing that changes after the liberation is your perception of self, the perception of who you think you are.

In a couple of years after a person is born, he begins to understand that he is an individual who is totally separate from the universe. He starts to develop an identity for himself as a person. He learns to distinguish between what is his and what is not his. He begins to think and say, 'this is my body', 'this is my opinion', 'this is my thought' etc. He first starts to create an identity based on his parents. 'This is my mom', 'this is my dad', 'this is my home', 'This is my school' and the list goes on like this.

This categorization is very important for human survival. In the process, he also develops two selfs: The 'actual self' that he thinks he is and 'the ideal self', the self that he wishes to be. For example, let us assume that a boy is not good in playing a game. He knows he is not good at it but he wants to be somebody who is good at it. In the pursuit of becoming good at it, at one point he may already start believing that he is good at it. Now, he adopts a new belief about himself, "I am getting better than my friends in playing this game".

As years go by, he develops many such beliefs about himself. He thinks about himself a lot and begins to mentally define who he is. He develops an image which now becomes very important to protect. He also has an ideal self, a self that he wants to become. He may want to be known as a rich, famous, intelligent, handsome or talented person. Everyone wants to be known and to be described as a successful person in life. Everyone wants to hear another person saying 'This guy is a lot better than his neighbor'.

In other words, every human being wants to become somebody. We already addressed this craving for becoming, in the first chapter. We want to protect and enhance the image of the self, the person in your head; we want to color it, decorate it, keep improving it and make it better than somebody else..

Human being develops this image using many other factors as well. He has a lot of ideologies, beliefs and worldviews that he identifies with. He derives an identity from it. He also derives the identity from his possessions, from knowledge that he gathered and even the experiences that he has gone through in his life.

The collection of all such beliefs about a person is the self-concept of the person. The image of the self that a person carries in his head, derives his identity from his past as well as from the dreams and hopes that he has about the future. This image needs constant protection and enhancement. Because of this need, everyone begins to participate in the rat race of the world, to show that he is better than at least someone else in someway. But the goals and themes differ among people. There may be someone who wants to do good things because he wants to be known as a good person. If someone calls him a jerk, selfish or dishonest, he may feel that as more insulting and threatening than being called as stupid, weak or poor.

How Real is this self?

If you observe your mind, you will see that all you notice is a constant flow of thoughts and sensations. Both Buddhism and Science agree that there is really no consistent, unchanging, solid self (the self with the lower case 's') that exists. This may be very hard to believe or accept because the idea of a separate individual is so deep rooted that you may consider this as a joke. It may even feel threatening because this self-concept is something that you always want to protect and enhance.

But this is true. According to neuroscience, your brain and your body is always in flux and there is no consistent self inside. But your thoughts flow very fast, often overlapping with each other without any gap, which give you a feeling that there is a solid self. These thoughts that arise so fast give you a feeling that the self is consistent.

Human beings have a tendency to treat ideas and other abstract concepts as concrete things. This is a deep rooted habit and is actually an error in our cognition. This is usually called Reification. The idea of a self or a person can be said as a deep rooted reification that we have developed over time. It has happened slowly and unconsciously ever since we first started to make the division of 'me' and the 'world'. Our perception of the reality gets completely clouded because of reification. Because of this, we don't really see the way things are.

It is not that this reification or this idea of the self is bad. Throughout this book, we are not discussing any moral rules or commandments. You are reading about a way to end your suffering and lead your life in a peaceful, fulfilled, liberated, conflictless, simple, natural and guilt-free way. This way doesn't require you to renounce your possessions, wealth or luxury. But it requires a renunciation of something else that you consider as the most important thing in your life: The idea of a seperate 'you' as a person.

In other words, liberation is a death of you as a person. Instead of being identified as a person, instead of putting a stamp of identity on the stream of your consciousness, it allows you to realize that you are actually existence itself. This will lead you to live your life while feeling boundless and free. But this renunciation of the self is not done in a forceful or merciless way. It happens by applying proper inquiry and practice. If you feel this threatening then you can take the Vedantic idea and identify yourself with the subject, the Self (note that there is a capital 'S')

So, let me give you a new attitude to deal with your mind and your body. Take sometime to observe your thoughts for a moment. The fact that you can observe the thoughts implies that you, the observer self is actually different from the thoughts. You are not your body either because you can observe it. You can feel every sensation of your body from inside.

Vedanta says that you are Brahman, you are the existence itself and in reality there is no separation. It is this deep rooted idea of a separate self which makes you feel that you are limited and separate from the reality. It is because of this separation that there is craving for fulfillment. And this separation can be permanently dissolved by proper instruction and practice.

There is a word called Adhyasa in Sanskrit, which means superimposition. When you take your mind, your body, your possessions etc as you or yours, you are actually taking something that is not really yourself and superimposing it on you. But you are actually the subject, not any of these objects which are witnessed by the subject. In other words, the object is superimposed on the subject and thus the subject is actually identified with the object.

Contemplate on the the following, which is an excerpt of what Buddha says in Anatta-Lakkhana sutta:

> "So, bhikkhus any kind of form whatever, whether past, future or presently arisen, whether gross or subtle, whether in oneself or external, whether inferior or superior, whether far or near, must with right understanding how it is, be

regarded thus: 'This is not mine, this is not I, this is not myself.'

Any kind of feeling whatever.. Any kind of perception whatever...Any kind of determination whatever... Any kind of consciousness whatever, whether past, future or presently arisen, whether gross or subtle, whether in oneself or external, whether inferior or superior, whether far or near must, with right understanding how it is, be regarded thus: 'This is not mine, this is not I, this is not my self.'

Bhikkhus, when a noble follower who has heard (the truth) sees thus, he finds estrangement in form, he finds estrangement in feeling, he finds estrangement in perception, he finds estrangement in determinations, he finds estrangement in consciousness.

When he finds estrangement, passion fades out. With the fading of passion, he is liberated. When liberated, there is knowledge that he is liberated."

- *"Anatta-lakkhana Sutta: The Discourse on the Not-self Characteristic" (SN 22.59), translated from the Pali by Ñanamoli Thera. Access to Insight (BCBS Edition), 13 June 2010,* http://www.accesstoinsight.org/tipitaka/sn/sn22/sn22.059 .nymo.html .

The above sutta (Buddhist verse) from Pali Canon is believed to be the second discourse delivered by Buddha. It is a very important sutta in Buddhism and is often quoted when talking about the doctrine of not-self.

The fact that you are not your thoughts will be obvious when the thoughts are not there at least for a few seconds. One way to do this is to practice observing your thoughts as if they have nothing to do with you. Within three to four months of such a practice that I did in 2002, I was able to experience a few moments without any thoughts.

Witnessing

So, let me give you something to practice. Sit in your chair and pay attention to your thought process. Don't try to think anything with your own effort but don't try to stop your thoughts either. Let thoughts arise and you just sit back and witness them. An attitude of detachment is necessary to do it properly. Don't judge any thought as good or bad. Assume that you are peeking into someone else's mind. Just observe each thought and be curious about the next thought or the bundle of thoughts that will arise. Even if you find yourself judging your own thoughts, recognize that as just another thought. You may forget this witnessing and get lost in the thought stream again and again. But don't feel guilty about it or feel that you failed. Because this is bound to happen again and again. But the key lies in recognizing that you missed the attention. As soon as you realize that you have forgotten to pay attention to the thought process, you will be back on track again. Along with your thoughts you can also pay attention to your body, if you have to move it for any reason. Let us call this practice 'Witnessing'. This method of Witnessing was recommended by Osho (Rajneesh) to his disciples.

It is important to maintain the attention moment to moment, without missing anything that is happening in your mind. When you forget, it is ok. But as soon as you realize that you have forgotten, bring your attention back to the thought process. You can do this practice whenever you are doing your daily activities like eating, walking, bathing, waiting in a queue etc. Extend this witnessing to your emotions as well. If you get angry, watch the anger arising in your body and feel it with attention. Pay moment to moment attention to the changes that it makes in your body and mind. Do the same for other emotions like sadness and fear. Allow the emotion to rise without resistance or suppression. Be mindful and watchful of those emotions as they gradually subside.

The problem with our minds is that we are lost in the thought process all the time. We are not consciousness that we are thinking. The tendency of mind is to go on in a continuous monologue, verbalize each and every thing that it comes across and always making some noise. When you pay attention to what the mind is doing, you stop giving the energy that the mind requires to continue the monologue. As you do it more and more, you will notice that the thought process is getting slowed down. Sometimes there might be even gaps in the thought process. You may have to wait for the second for the next thought to arise.

The practice that I just suggested has been recommended by many people before. For example, Buddha taught a meditation practice called mindfulness, which is nothing but watching the breath, thoughts and sensations moment to moment with a detached non-judgemental attitude while sitting with closed eyes. But when we do the same with open eyes as we are engaged in daily activities, it is witnessing. Witnessing is a way to integrate mindfulness into our daily lives. This way, our life itself becomes a spiritual practice and every moment becomes an opportunity.

As you do this everyday, pay attention to the unconscious thought patterns, pay attention to the games that your mind is playing and pay attention to the need to become as somebody. This is a very interesting practice and a powerful exploration of your own mind. As you bring awareness to the different layers of mind, you will become more and more peaceful.

J.Krishnamurthi called this practice as Choiceless awareness. Let us look at some of the excerpts from the talks he made in Bangalore on 4th July, 1948 :

> "Now, is the thinker different from his thoughts? Does the thinker exist without thoughts? Is there a thinker apart from thought? Stop thinking, and where is the thinker? Is the thinker of one thought different from the thinker of another thought? Is the thinker separate from his thought, or does thought create the thinker, who then identifies himself with thought when he finds it convenient, and separates himself

when it is not convenient? That is, what is the "I", the thinker? Obviously, the thinker is composed of various thoughts which have become identified as the "me". So, the thoughts produce the thinker, not the other way round. If I have no thoughts, then there is no thinker; not that the thinker is different each time, but if there are no thoughts there is no thinker. So, thoughts produce the thinker, as actions produce the actor. The actor does not produce actions.

Audience: You seem to suggest, Sir, that by ceasing to think, the "I" will be absent.

Krishnamurti: The I is made up of my qualities, my idiosyncrasies, my passions, my possessions, my house, my money, my wife, my books. These create the idea of "me", I do not create them. Do you agree?"

- *(from http://jiddu-krishnamurti.net)*

Here, the thinker that J.Krishnamurti is referring to is the person who you think you are. It is the image that you carry in your head about yourself, which derives its identity from the story of the past and the hopes and dreams of the future. But there is really no such person when there are no thoughts. All that exists in the absence of the thoughts is just pure awareness, the subject. Since the thoughts move so fast, the constant movement of the thought process gives you the illusion of a separate and consistent self.

The Three Marks of Existence

Buddha called three characteristics as three marks of existence: suffering (dukkha), impermanence (anicca) and not-self (anatta).

When you witness your own mind or the external world, all you see is the ever changing phenomenon of Maya, the constant flux of Prakriti, the incessant movements of objects which also includes your thoughts, emotions, sensations etc. This is what he called as impermanence. And this is also inherently empty of a self. When we take a closer look, all we see is different aggregates and not a self. We see thoughts floating around, emotions bubbling up and sensation crawling over, which keep changing each and every moment. Clinging to these aggregates and trying to hold them together is what creates suffering.

In Gestalt psychology, the fallacy of reification in our normal perception is explained by taking the following image as an example:

Do you see a triangle in the picture A and a sphere in picture B? A quick glance may tell you that they exist. But if you look closer at these pictures, all you see is some independent pieces in black that give you an illusion that there is an image of a sphere and an image of a triangle. The same way, you see some disparate shapes in the pictures C and D, but you see them as belonging to a single shape. But the truth is, this image is 'empty' of those shapes. The same way, Buddha says that all you notice in your mind is a flux of impermanent and ever changing thoughts, emotions and sensations and they are inherently empty of a self. When you practice witnessing, you need to see your thought process, sensations and perceptions as they are, as separate aggregates and see how they are actually not 'you' or 'yours'. Clinging to these aggregates and identifying with them causes suffering.

You may have noticed that as a person you always want to be consistent. Because of this consistency, you may sometimes deny one part of yours. For example, let us say you want to become a celibate monk and you now believe that you have renounced your sexual desires. You may consider yourself as someone who doesn't have desires because that has always been an ideal self that you wanted to become. You may repress your desires for a while, divert your attention as much as possible from lust and slowly begin to believe that those desires have disappeared. You may be a proud monk now and hold an image of yourself that is similar to a saint. You may also try to repress this pride because you have been always taught to be humble. But your hormones don't know any of that. They never check with you before they begin to start their work nor they care to give you attendance. When you finally fail and give in to the impulses of your hormones you not only feel ashamed but you can't tolerate this inconsistency. Even if you successfully control your impulses, you will still feel a discomfort because of encountering a desire that contradicts with the belief that you have about yourself.

There is a term in Psychology called Cognitive dissonance. This is a mental discomfort that you experience while you perform an action that contradicts with the belief that you have already, especially when the belief is about yourself. You may also experience cognitive dissonance when you encounter facts that contradict with your previous beliefs. Cognitive dissonance happens because of your efforts to maintain a consistent self when such a thing doesn't exist. One symptom of a liberated life is that you will be free of cognitive dissonance after it happens.

These three marks of existence namely impermanence, not-self and suffering is something that needs to be clearly seen and understood by making inquiry on our totality of our conscious experience as often as you can. You need to have a clear understanding of the subject and the object, so that you can make such an inquiry and also practice witnessing with perfection. But keep this inquiry and witnessing separate and don't practice both at the same time.

Chapter Five: The Common Barriers and Traps in the Spiritual Path

Beleifs

Spirituality is often associated with religion and both of them are often discussed together. While a religion is fundamentally based on beliefs, the spiritual path actually doesn't require any beliefs. In fact, in my experience, beliefs have always been barriers.

What exactly is a belief? When you think something as true, which doesn't have any factual certainty yet, it is a belief. In other words, it is actually a pretension. You pretend that you know something but you actually don't. Beliefs, especially when religious have caused a lot of violence and destruction in the world. But we have been always threatened to believe in things right from our childhood by saying that non-believers will go to eternal hell. When beliefs become deep rooted, our thinking becomes biased and fallacious. We also start to derive our identity and get some solace from beliefs. This not only stops us from seeing thing the way they are, but this also works against the pursuit of liberation by strengthening the idea of a separate self.

This doesn't mean that we shouldn't have any assumptions about anything. Sometimes it may be necessary to make assumptions. But it is very important to treat assumptions as just assumptions. You should be honest to yourself that you don't know what is true. When we believe in those assumptions and actually take them as facts, we will start talking about our beliefs with others as well. This becomes one more factor that gives us an identity. We begin to own those beliefs and start calling them 'mine'.. Then you start to think 'This is what I think and I am right'. Your mind will engage in defending these beliefs because they are now yours.

A search for any kind of knowledge begins by realizing that you don't know the answer for it. If you believe in some baseless answer that somebody gave you and become satisfied with it, you will never know what is true. It may give you something to identify with and give you some solace, but it will stop you from actually knowing the truth.

Here is what Buddha says in Kalama sutta:

> "Do not go upon what has been acquired by repeated hearing; nor upon tradition; nor upon rumor; nor upon what is in a scripture; nor upon surmise; nor upon an axiom; nor upon specious reasoning; nor upon a bias towards a notion that has been pondered over; nor upon another's seeming ability; nor upon the consideration, 'The monk is our teacher.' "

- *"Kalama Sutta: The Buddha's Charter of Free Inquiry",* translated from the Pali by Soma Thera. *Access to Insight (BCBS Edition), 30 November 2013,* http://www.accesstoinsight.org/lib/authors/soma/wheel008.html

First he says, 'Do not go upon what has been acquired by repeated hearing'. When you hear something over and over again, you start to believe in it. Psychologists call this as 'The illusory truth effect'. It can be defined as the tendency of our mind to believe in anything after we are exposed to it repeatedly. A study done in 1977 in Temple University near Philadelphia, confirmed this as a fact . This study was published in Journal of Verbal Learning & Verbal Behaviour with the title 'Frequency and the conference of referential validity'. (Hasher L, Goldstein D, Toppino T - 1977).

Even though the phenomena of illusory truth effect has been established as a scientific fact only in the last few decades, people have already known it throughout centuries. Buddha must have observed this tendency too. Many people in the field of politics, advertising and even cult leaders have taken advantage of this fact to make people to believe in false information. You may think you are smart and this will never happen to you, but this is really something that happens to almost everyone, no matter how intelligent they are.

Buddha further says "nor upon tradition; nor upon rumor; nor upon what is in a scripture; nor upon surmise"

Just because something is traditionally believed to be true, it doesn't have to be true. When someone argues something is true just because the tradition says so, it is a fallacy called 'Appeal to tradition'. But we witness the unfortunate truth of people believing in a lot of strange things just because the belief is traditional. Buddha says that no matter how old the tradition is, don't go ahead and blindly believe what it says.

Next thing Buddha talks about is the belief based upon rumors. This can be compared to 'Appeal to popularity', the tendency of believing in something just because many people believe so. Of course, rumors may not be believed by the majority. But still, believing in rumors and believing in a popular belief is based on the same concept: You believe in something because others believe so.

There is a Chinese proverb: "Three men make a tiger". There is an interesting story behind it which is described in a Chinese text 'Zhan Guo Ce' written sometime during 5th- 3rd centuries BCE. The story goes like this: Pang Cong, an official of the state of Wei was about to leave the country for a trip. Before leaving he asked the King of Wei, "Will you believe if someone reports to you that a tiger is roaming in the capital city?". The King said 'No'. Pang Cong asked him again, "Will you believe if two people report it?". The king started to think. After a long pause, Pang Cong asked again, "What if three people say so?". The King replied that he would believe if that was the case. Pang Cong then said to the King "Even though a tiger roaming in a busy market in the capital city sounds absurd, it sounds believable if it is reported by three people. I have more than three opponents and critics, So in case they spread rumors about me, don't believe it!"

Buddha also says "Don't believe in something just because scriptures say so! Don't believe in something if there is no evidence to support it." He also talks about biased notions which we will discuss shortly. Note that Buddha also says not to blindly believe in something just because a teacher or a spiritual authority says so.

It is also important to not to believe our own thoughts and take them seriously. This attitude will be very useful for non-judgmentally witnessing your mind. Today a thought may pop up in your mind which says 'I am ugly'. By reacting to this thought, you may become sad or even depressed. Tomorrow the same mind of yours may produce another thought 'I am looking good!'. When you take this seriously, it will strengthen the identification you have with your looks. Again, it is not that trying to look good is bad, but your well being should not depend on looking good.. If you are identified with anything as you or yours, it is prone to cause suffering. But you can't force yourself to not to identify with things. The identification slowly falls of by itself as you do the witnessing practice more and more.

Possibility and Certainty

There are certain things which we think as possibilities. We are not certain about the fact but we still know that it is possible. Even though we don't know for sure, we discover that it is actually possible and probable.

Let me give you an example. Scientists are searching for alien life because they understand that there is a possibility that there is life in the other places of this universe. But this is an assumption based on inference. Now, if somebody shows you a distant star and asks you, 'Do you think there is life on the planets revolving around that star'?, you may say that it is possible. But is it certain? No! This is the difference between a possibility and certainty. This is an important distinction to keep in mind.

The reason I mention this is because people always cling to one possibility that support their beliefs. They never look at all the possibilities and give equal importance to them. And this is a fallacy that we need to watch out for. The reason you do that is because you are identified with a certain belief, derive a sense of identity from it, you develop a need to justify the belief and prove that it is true and you only consider the possibility that seems to support your belief.

Let us say that you call your crush and she doesn't answer. You text her and you don't get a reply. There may be many possible reasons for this. Her phone may be in silent, she is away from her phone, the television volume in the phone is too loud to hear the ringing of the phone, she is too busy to even bother to look who is calling, her phone got stolen, she went out but forgot to take the phone with her or she is ignoring your call. But let us say that you already believe that she is not interested in you. Then you will only consider the last possibility and conclude with certainty that she is really ignoring you. But this shows a bias because you only consider one probability and drawing your conclusions based on that. You then mistake a probability for certainty.

The reason why we do this is because we want to maintain a consistent self. We want to be right all the time. The attachment to a separate self automatically creates a need to protect it. Be alert and watchful when such things happen in your mind and make sure you witness those thoughts while doing the witnessing meditation . The more you notice such unconscious behaviours of mind, the more you will disidentify with your mind. You can make a good progress by watching the thought patterns that strive to protect your identity or assert your superiority. But remember not to judge those thoughts. If judgemental thoughts arise, let them also arise and pass away like the passing clouds in the sky. You just need to maintain a steady stream of awareness and notice these thoughts with acceptance. Remind yourself often by realizing how these thoughts are not 'you'.

Ego - What is it?

The word ego has many meanings. You need to watch out for the problem with the words that we discussed earlier, whenever you hear or read anything about ego. Let us look at the dictionary meaning. The simplest definition would be 'a person's sense of self-esteem or self-importance'.

We can say that it is a function. It constantly functions to defend, assert, enhance and improve the self and the self-concept. When you practice witnessing, it is very important to observe how ego functions and how it always wants to be right, how it defends and rationalizes your beliefs and behaviour. As your witnessing goes deeper, sharp and unwavering, you, as a person will feel like becoming less and less and finally disappear. But it needs long time practice.

It is very useful to know about the defense mechanisms, the strategies employed by ego to defend yourself or justify your thoughts and behaviours. In psychoanalytic theory, defence mechanisms are psychological strategies brought into action by the unconscious mind to manipulate, deny, or distort reality in order to defend against feelings of anxiety and unacceptable impulses and to maintain one's self concept. When you practice witnessing, observe whenever such defense mechanisms arises.

The following are some of the common defence mechanisms:

(From the Wiki article for Defence mechanisms at https://en.wikipedia.org/wiki/Defence_mechanisms)

1. Repression - Burying or suppressing a thought because it causes anxiety or cognitive dissonance. We already discussed about repression and its consequences. When you witness your mind, instead of burying a thought, allow the thought to fully arise and pass away while you give your fullest alert attention to it. Treat that thought with a sense of acceptance.

2. Identification - This is something that we are discussing right from the beginning, which is also considered as one of the defense mechanisms.

3. Rationalization - Justifying your behaviour and motivations by substituting good and acceptable reasons for the actual motivations.

4. Splitting: seeing something or someone as either all good or all bad. Almost everyone has it. You always think a person as either all good or all bad. but in reality, he is just like any other human being acting in various ways during various times, depending on his nature and nurture.

5. Idealization: Tendency to perceive another person as having more desirable qualities than the person may actually have.

6. Wishful thinking: Formation of beliefs and making decisions according to what might be pleasing to imagine instead of by appealing to evidence, rationality, or reality. It is a fallacy in our reasoning which has a form 'I wish that P is true/false, therefore P is true/false'.

If you think about your behaviour and thought processes in the past, you may be able to recollect many instances when your ego employed any of the above defence mechanisms. When you become aware of these unconscious tendencies, recognize them perfectly and catch hold of them as they arise, it is a good indication that your witnessing practice has deepened.

Once a person is liberated, the ego will still function and it may retain just a little bit of defensive nature but there is really no clinging or identification with the self-concept. You will not really have a solid self concept at all. You may just derive a subtle sense of self for the purpose of interaction with the world. But it will only arise when it is needed. The self-concept after liberation hardly has any content and this self-concept is then just a small piece of information derived from long term memory to working memory for the sole purpose of interaction with the world. But there is no consistency, continuity or a solid sense of self. Liberation removes almost all of the self-referential thinking.

Cognitive Biases

We think that we are rational human beings and that we are making conclusions based on perfect logic and reasoning. But there are many errors in our reasoning and cognition which are common for all human beings. A cognitive bias is an error in our thinking which makes us deviate from norm or rationality in judgment and decision making.

There are a lot of reasons for various cognitive biases that we have. But many of them do stem from the need to make ourselves seem or look better than what we actually are. The attachment to the self-concept tends to make us believe that we are always right and makes us to judge situations, people according to the version of social reality that we have created ourselves in our mind. Being aware of some important cognitive biases can be very helpful. Once you are aware of them, you can notice the way your thinking is biased, as you observe them in witnessing meditation. It is very helpful in developing insight about the tendencies of our minds and easily identify them.

Cognitive bias is an important subject. Learning about the biases can not only help you towards liberation but can also help you in your daily life in various ways when you try to make judgements or decisions. I think lessons about cognitive biases should be included in the textbooks of high school children so that they are aware of such tendencies in our thought process. In this section, I will name and explain the most common cognitive biases.

Cognitive biases can persist even after liberation. But their effect is not much in people who are liberated. It is also easy for them to notice such bias in their thinking and make sure that their decisions or judgements are not influenced by bias.

Confirmation bias

This is the king of biases. Your beliefs define much of your identity and self-concept. Confirmation bias is the result of the influence these beliefs have on your thought process. Confirmation bias causes the following problems:

1. You always search for things in a way that conforms your pre-existing beliefs.
2. You favor the information which are in line with your pre-existing beliefs.
3. You pay more attention to, remember and recall the information easily when the information supports your pre-existing beliefs.
4. You also interpret things according to your pre-existing beliefs.

We already discussed the issue about people favoring one possibility among all the possibilities. Confirmation bias is the reason why they do this. When your thoughts are clouded with confirmation bias, you will interpret ambiguous evidence as supporting your beliefs. Your beliefs may continue even if you are presented with a clear evidence that shows that your belief is wrong. This is also known as belief perseverance.

Leo Tolstoy, in his essay 'What is Art?' says the following:

"I know that most men—not only those considered clever, but even those who are very clever, and capable of understanding most difficult scientific, mathematical, or philosophic problems—can very seldom discern even the simplest and most obvious truth if it be such as to oblige them to admit the falsity of conclusions they have formed, perhaps with much difficulty—conclusions of which they are proud, which they have taught to others, and on which they have built their lives."

- Tolstoy, Leo. What is Art? p. 124 (1899).

Confirmation bias doesn't happen intentionally. You may not have any intention to deceive yourself and others and you may not at all be aware that your thinking is biased. Unless you have the ability to non-judgmentally observe your minds, you may not notice it.

Fundamental attribution error

When you notice someone being very angry, you may not think much about the situational factors that caused his anger. Instead, you may be very quick to label him as 'short tempered guy'. But if you yourself are angry, you may say that situational factors caused your anger. Fundamental attribution bias is a tendency to place undue emphasis on the internal qualities of other people when you explain other people's behaviour.

You may have also noticed this: When you succeed in anything, you have a tendency to attribute the success to your own abilities. But when there is a failure, you tend to blame the situational factors. This is a related bias, known as self-serving bias. This is done to show yourself to you and others in a way that is favorable to your self-esteem. In other words, your reasoning is distorted by the need of protecting and enhancing your self concept. Both fundamental attribution error and self-serving bias are the two subsets or aspects of a single phenomenon called actor-observer bias.

Bandwagon Effect

When you adopt a belief very quickly because a lot of people believe in it, it can be said as bandwagon effect. People always want to think and behave like most of the others in the society. They always want to conform to the standards and norms of other people around them. This is the reason why many people believe many things without questioning. When nobody else questions those beliefs, you also tend to follow the herd.

Authority bias

Authority bias is the tendency to attribute greater accuracy to anything that is said by an authority figure. This is the reason why people tend to believe everything that scriptures and teachers say. You also tend to obey the orders and follow the commandments of authority figure.

Bias blind spot

Bias blind spot is the lack of the ability to observe and accept one's own biases. Generally, people tend to think that others are more biased than themselves. This is again a self deception that happens because of our intention to view ourselves in a positive light.

If you think about all these biases that we discussed, we can say that a lot of our biases are the product of clinging to the self-concept and our pursuit of protecting and enhancing it. These biases happen unconsciously and without your deliberate intention. The more you bring your unconscious thought processes to your conscious and mindful attention, the easier it would be to recognize and avoid these biases.

Learning to Live with Uncertainty

Here is a secret to know anything quickly and precisely than you normally would.. It is to have an attitude 'I don't know'...And this is recommended in spiritual seeking as well.

There is a problem in human mind. It cannot live with uncertainty. Because, uncertainty is uncomfortable and also undesirable to ego. A false verbal statement can actually satisfy this uncertainty. That is why many people are satisfied when they are told that God created the world in a week. Because, now they know and they are certain.

This is what leads to all kinds of beliefs. And these beliefs stop us from actually knowing the truth. This is exactly the reason why we believe our thoughts and take them too seriously. Sometimes we quickly attribute certain qualities to other people, thinking 'he is arrogant', 'she is stupid', 'he is dishonest' etc (fundamental attribution error). Once a person gets these thoughts, he actually believes these thoughts; In future, this leads him to believe in only those statements which actually agree with the previous beliefs (confirmation bias).

Beliefs don't stop with these things alone. People form beliefs on how their emotional state or the state of well being is going to be solely based on the current emotional state or the current level of well being. That is called Projection bias. Also, it is due to this bias that people sometimes have beliefs on how an enlightened person's state of mind will be. It is also because of this that some people don't believe in enlightenment at all. Just because suffering is unavoidable now, they think they can't be free of suffering forever.

But all these beliefs stop people from knowing. Sometimes we form our beliefs based on an authority, sometimes a beloved one, sometimes based on a book etc. Then we start to argue what we believe is correct. It is not so easy for ego to see a contradiction in the beliefs of the mind which it thinks it owns.

It doesn't mean that we should completely reject whatever we hear, read or think. There is a third choice, to just let it be as a memory or as a possible hypothesis, without coming to a conclusion. Because once we have come to a conclusion, we have closed all the doors of knowing anything further.

The whole approach of science is based on this. With a scientific approach, you don't believe in anything. And you don't come to a quick conclusion based on a very weak evidence. Even if you do come to a conclusion, you become open minded to change it if a new observation challenges the earlier conclusion. A true seeker is actually a scientist of the inner world.

Just to let you know, even a liberated person has beliefs and his thinking may be biased to a certain extent. Those beliefs are restricted to things in general and not usually related to the person himself. With liberation, there is a permanent detachment from beliefs. You stop owning the beliefs after liberation. But those beliefs are still in memory and have not been worked on. But after liberation, it is a lot easier to see through one's beliefs and biases.

Spiritual Ego

This is the worst trap that spiritual seekers can fall into. Because of the craving to enrich the self concept and the desire to solidify, maintain and enhance our conceptual self, your ego always attempts to derive a sense of identity from your own spiritual progress. Your self concept tries to persist in a new way and you can recognize this when you ever find yourself thinking 'I am becoming more spiritual', 'I am going to be enlightened', 'I am more smart and intelligent than others because the people around me don't know what I know' etc.

Our tendency to identify, categorize things as 'mine' and 'not mine' and try to portray or show ourselves in a positive light is something that we need to always watch out for. When you get thoughts that reveal this tendency, remember to do the following:

1. Recognize the thought for what it is and accept the fact that such a thought arises, without feeling guilty or feeling that you have failed. In case you feel guilty or judgemental about the thought, witness that feeling and any thought that arises out of that feeling. When it comes to witnessing, each thought is an opportunity.

2. Witness the thoughts with objectivity and non-judgemental attitude and realize that those thoughts are not you.. Realize that those thoughts are not self.

3. Wait for the thought to pass away on its own, keep paying attention and curiously wait for the next thought to arise and repeat the process.

Many people who are new to spiritual path get very excited. When you understand what exactly we are trying to do in a spiritual path, you start to wonder how awesome it is. You may be interested to tell other people about it. Everyone goes through such a period. Let us call it 'spiritual honeymoon' period.

People sometimes indulge in nasty things when they are in this spiritual honeymoon period. They unconsciously develop a feeling that now they are superior to the rest of the population. They may indulge in judging other people, comment about how idiotic, unconscious or ignorant certain people are and they may even start giving spiritual advices to other people. They may start parroting what their guru says and become obsessive in defending their gurus. All these behaviours arise because of the tendency of our mind to save the self concept. Your mind doesn't want to let it go and doesn't want to disidentify from it. Instead, it tries to use the spiritual path itself as a way to enhance the self-concept. Beware of this trap! Many people get trapped at this stage and remain like this for their lifetime.

Liberation is not an accomplishment. It is not a goal of a personal self. So, you can't really say that you are ambitious about liberation. In other words, no one actually gets liberated or enlightened because the idea of a 'someone' disappears with liberation. Once you step on the spiritual path, you always need to remind yourself to watch out for the thoughts which try to associate your spiritual practice with superiority or nobleness. As you bring more and more non-judgemental awareness to these thoughts as soon as they arise, these tendencies will lose their power.

Chapter Six: The Spiritual Practice

It is time to actually talk about the practice - what exactly you need to do. We have already discussed witnessing, which is something that has to be integrated in everything you do. The beauty of the witnessing process is that it doesn't require a specific time to be allocated. In this chapter, we will go into the details of the actual practice. I will also suggest some independent practices which are supplementary and which require a specific time to be allocated.

There is something that needs to be addressed before we proceed. If you already have some familiarity with spiritual traditions or teachers, you may have heard them saying 'You can't do anything to be enlightened'. It doesn't mean that you should not put any effort into the whole process. What it means is this: Even though you do certain things for liberation, liberation itself is the annihilation of the thought or idea that 'I am the doer'. When you take the subject or the observer self as you, you are already liberated. Even though the idea of a separate self with an independant doership is an illusion which causes bondage, the feeling that you are bound or not liberated in itself is an illusion. Because, when there is no separate 'you', who is there to be liberated? You as the subject and the observer is already free.

But the statement that you are already liberated doesn't seem to be experientially true now. That is why there is suffering and dissatisfaction. The whole work is to remove the idea that 'I am a separate self and hence I am trapped'. Liberation removes both these ideas: It removes the hard-wired idea that you are separate from existence. Thus, it also removes the idea that there is actually someone who is trapped and who has to be liberated'. It is a paradox, so don't spend too much time in resolving the paradox and don't get confused when you hear such teachings. The point is to always remember that whatever practice that you are doing will not directly cause liberation but it works to remove the idea that there is bondage.

Remember this analogy: When the clouds move away, movement of clouds do not create the sun; The sun did not come into being because the clouds moved away. But the disappearance of the clouds revealed the sun which was already there all along. The same way, whatever practice that we do is to remove the impurities which are clouding the truth of who you are. The practice removes the idea that there is a doer. The idea that there is a separate self which is the doer of actions is actually like a thick sheet of clouds which is stopping you from seeing the truth.

Witnessing and Karma Yoga

In Indian tradition, there is a concept called Karma Yoga. Karma Yoga is generally considered by many as a standalone spiritual path. Vedanta considers karma yoga as a stepping stone to the actual spiritual practice and the way to develop prerequisites such as viveka (discrimination between the subject and the object) and non-attachment. But Karma Yoga is one of the widely misunderstood topics. Usually, Karma Yoga is defined as doing your actions while surrendering the fruits of action to God. But people interpret this in their own ways.

Let me give you the basic idea behind Karma Yoga. Usually your actions are treated by you as a means to an end. You do something because you are attached to the fruit of action, something that will happen in the future. So, throughout your action and after your action is completed, you tend to live in the future and dwell on thoughts about the fruits of action. This takes you away from the present moment. But if you do your actions with full awareness while being fully present, the action itself becomes a spiritual practice.

Attachment is a product of identification: clinging to the aggregates and deriving a sense of self from them. Karma Yoga helps you to develop non-attachment. But non-attachment is not uninvolvement. You can fully involve in an action and do it more lovingly when you are not attached to the fruit of action.

You need two things to accomplish this:

1. Surrender: Here, the word 'surrender' doesn't mean surrendering to a person. It means surrendering to the existence itself, without resisting what is. Whatever happens in this moment right now is something that cannot be avoided. You can possibly avoid or change what will happen

in the next moment; but whatever that is happening right now is already happening. There is no point in fighting with it. So, what happens at this moment has to be accepted without resistance. This attitude of acceptance and not resisting to what is happening is surrender.

2. Being in the present moment: Being fully present is being mindful. Being mindful is nothing but witnessing. When you witness your body and mind as you do an action, your attention is fully in the present moment.

In Psychology, there is a term called intrinsic motivation. With extrinsic motivation, we do actions because they help us to get something that is pleasant or to avoid something that is unpleasant. But with intrinsic motivation, we do certain things because doing those activities itself brings us joy. When you go for a morning walk to reduce weight, your action is done out of extrinsic motivation. But when you go for a walk because you enjoying walking in early morning, it is done out of intrinsic motivation.

When you do all of your daily activities with intrinsic motivation, it becomes karma yoga. You can really enjoy what you are doing, when you surrender the idea that 'You are the doer' and do everything mindfully, without worrying about the fruits of action. We really don't have to call it as 'Karma yoga' and categorize it as something separate. It all boils down to witnessing. When you integrate witnessing into your daily activities, you are automatically practicing Karma yoga.

Witnessing - In Osho's words

When I was about 20 years old, I learnt the art of witnessing by reading and listening to the talks of Osho. Osho was a very controversial and influential person. I will talk more about Osho in a different chapter and I will explain about his methods as well as all the controversies around him. Here, I would like to include an excerpt from Osho's talks which is about witnessing. This will help you to get a clear idea about it:

"Just be, and watch. Being is not doing, and watching is also not doing. You sit silently doing nothing, witnessing whatsoever is happening. Thoughts will be moving in your mind; your body may be feeling some tension somewhere, you may have a migraine. Just be a witness. Don't be identified with it. Watch, be a watcher on the hills, and everything else is happening in the valley. It is a knack, not an art.

Meditation is not a science. It is not an art, it is a knack – just that way. All that you need is a little patience.

The old habits will continue; the thoughts will go on rushing. And your mind is always in a rush hour, the traffic is always jammed. Your body is not accustomed to sitting silently – you will be tossing and turning. Nothing to be worried about. Just watch that the body is tossing and turning, that the mind is whirling, is full of thoughts – consistent, inconsistent, useless – fantasies, dreams. You remain in the center, just watching.

All the religions of the world have taught people to do something: stop the process of thought, force the body into a still posture. That's what yoga is – a long practice of forcing the body to be still. But a forced body is not still. And all the prayers, concentrations, contemplations of all the religions do the same with the mind: they force it, they don't allow the thoughts to move. Yes, you have the capacity to do it. And if you persist you may be able to stop the thought process. But this is not the real thing, it is absolutely fake.

When stillness comes on its own, when silence descends without your effort, when you watch thoughts and a moment comes when thoughts start disappearing and silence starts happening, that is beautiful. The thoughts stop of their own accord if you don't identify, if you remain a witness and you don't say, "This is my thought."

You don't say, "This is bad, this is good," "This should be there...." and "This should not be there...." Then you are not a watcher; you have prejudices, you have certain attitudes. A watcher has no prejudice, he has no judgment. He simply sees like a mirror.

When you bring something in front of a mirror it reflects, simply reflects. There is no judgment that the man is ugly, that the man is beautiful, that, "Aha! What a good nose you have got." The mirror has nothing to say. Its nature is to mirror; it mirrors. This is what I call meditation: you simply mirror everything within or without.

And I guarantee you.... I can guarantee because it has happened to me and to many of my people; just watching patiently – maybe a few days will pass, maybe a few months, maybe a few years. There is no way of saying because each individual has a different collection.

You must have seen people collecting antiques, postal stamps. Everybody has a different collection; the quantity may be different, hence the time it takes will be different – but go on remaining a witness as much as you can. And this meditation needs no special time. You can wash the floor and remain silently watching yourself washing the floor.

I can move my hand unconsciously, without watching, or I can move it with full awareness. And there is a qualitative difference. When you move it unconsciously it is mechanical. When you move it with consciousness there is grace. Even in the hand, which is part of your body, you will feel silence, coolness – what to say about the mind?

With your watching and watching, slowly the rush of thoughts starts getting less and less. Moments of silence start appearing; a thought comes, and then there is silence before another thought appears. These gaps will give you the first glimpse of meditation and the first joy that you are arriving home.

Soon the gaps will be bigger, and finally the gap is always with you. You may be doing something, the silence is there. You may not be doing anything, the silence is there. Even in sleep the silence is there."

- Osho, *From the False to the Truth, Talk #3*

Witnessing is the core of the spiritual path that we are discussing in this book. As your witnessing deepens, you will be able to witness even subtle feelings and mental states with complete detachment. The speed of your involuntary thought process will reduce and your mind will get lighter and lighter. You may start noticing gaps between thoughts and during those gaps, you will simply exist as pure awareness.

Witnessing and the State of Flow

As your witnessing deepens and once you get the first momentary glimpse of being as pure awareness without any thoughts, you may develop a tendency to automatically enter into the states of flow. The state of flow can be defined as being fully immersed in a feeling of energized focus, full involvement, and enjoyment in the process of doing an activity. There is a complete absorption in what you do which results in a loss in your sense of space and time.

Mihaly Csikszentmihalyi, a Hungarian psychologist was the one who coined the word 'flow'. When he noticed some painters who were immersed in their work and even disregard their need for food and sleep, he started to wonder what could be the reason for this. After some detailed research, the concept of flow was discovered.

In an interview with Wired magazine, this is how Mihaly Csikszentmihalyi defined 'flow':

"Being completely involved in an activity for its own sake. The ego falls away. Time flies. Every action, movement, and thought follows inevitably from the previous one, like playing jazz. Your whole being is involved, and you're using your skills to the utmost."

Flow is an optimal state of intrinsic motivation. In other words, it is an optimal state of Karma Yoga. During the states of flow, the subject and object merge and become one. But this is not the same as getting lost in thoughts and becoming identified with them. Usually, flow states are experienced along with a tremendous reduction in involuntary thought process.

Catharsis and Dynamic Meditation

In the pursuit of becoming the ideal self, we have repressed many emotions and buried them in the unconscious. Because of this, we haven't adequately expressed or experienced those emotions. This repressing of emotions has made our minds heavy and have added a deep pile of unconscious under the thin layer of our conscious minds. Before we make any progress in the spiritual path, we need to clean up a lot of the repressed emotions. Catharsis is a process that can help accomplish this.

Catharsis is based on a theory called 'Hydraulic theory of emotions'. If the water flow in the pipe is stopped, a pressure can build up inside the pipe. The same way, the theory says that if emotions are not released, they can build up inside our mind and cause various problems. There is also another theory called 'reservoir theory' which says that whenever we repress emotions like anger, it is stored up in our unconscious, similar to how a reservoir stores up water. Unless the repressed emotions are released, the reservoir keeps growing and can lead to unpleasant consequences. Catharsis allows these repressed emotions to find release.

Many psychologists challenge the concept behind catharsis and question its effectiveness. They have also questioned the hydraulic theory of emotions. Many studies have actually shown the opposite effect for catharsis. There have been cases where the emotional problems became worse after catharsis. This is especially true if the patient has gone through a really bad trauma. So, when it comes to scientific evidence, neither hydraulic theory nor reservoir theory has any substantial evidence.

But catharsis is still accepted by many psychotherapists as an useful practice. I have personally found it very useful. But there is a basic difference between the kind of catharsis that psychotherapists use and the one that I have practiced. Psychotherapists often encourage the clients to recollect a bad experience from past and relive the emotions. But when we recollect anything, brain makes those recollections stronger. But when I did cathartic practices, I did not recollect any long forgotten memories. Instead, I just used it to vent any emotions that I had been having lately.

Thomas J. Scheff, a Professor of Dept of Sociology at UCSB emphasized cognitive awareness which he called 'distancing. According to him, only if there is a distance between the observer and the emotions, only when you witness your emotions as a passive observer, catharsis is effective. The person going through catharsis should maintain the observer role instead of maintaining the role of a participant. So, expressing emotions in a proper catharsis is not the same as expressing the emotion in isolation, in everyday life. The important concept of catharsis is awareness; the success of catharsis depends on how much mindful we are and how much detached we are from the mental processes.

Catharsis is a component in the dynamic meditation developed by Osho. Dynamic meditation is a very powerful practice. It has five stages. It is very important to maintain steady awareness and be a witness throughout the entire session. Witnessing is an important aspect of dynamic meditation.

Here is what Osho says about dynamic meditation:

> "This is a meditation in which you have to be continuously alert, conscious, aware, whatsoever you do. The first step, breathing; the second step, catharsis; the third step, the mantra, 'Hoo.' Remain a witness. Don't get lost. It is easy to get lost. While you are breathing you can forget; you can become one with the breathing so much that you can forget the witness. But then you miss the point. Breathe as fast, as deep as possible, bring your total energy to it, but still remain a witness. Observe what is happening as if you are just a spectator, as if the whole thing is happening to somebody else, as if the whole thing is happening in the body and the consciousness is just centered and looking. This witnessing has to be carried in all the three steps. And when everything stops, and in the fourth step you have become completely inactive, frozen, then this alertness will come to its peak."

Below are the instructions for Dynamic meditation as given in Osho.com:

> "*Instructions:*
>
> The meditation lasts one hour and has five stages. Keep your eyes closed throughout, using a blindfold if necessary. It can be done alone, and can be even more powerful if it is done with others.
>
> *First Stage: 10 minutes*

Breathing chaotically through the nose, let breathing be intense, deep, fast, without rhythm, with no pattern – and concentrating always on the exhalation. The body will take care of the inhalation. The breath should move deeply into the lungs. Do this as fast and as hard as you possibly can until you literally become the breathing. Use your natural body movements to help you to build up your energy. Feel it building up, but don't let go during the first stage.

Second Stage: 10 minutes

EXPLODE! ... Let go of everything that needs to be thrown out. Follow your body. Give your body freedom to express whatever is there. Go totally mad. Scream, shout, cry, jump, kick, shake, dance, sing, laugh; throw yourself around. Hold nothing back; keep your whole body moving. A little acting often helps to get you started. Never allow your mind to interfere with what is happening. Consciously go mad. Be total.

Third Stage: 10 minutes

With arms raised high above your head, jump up and down shouting the mantra, "Hoo! Hoo! Hoo!" as deeply as possible. Each time you land, on the flats of your feet, let the sound hammer deep into the sex center. Give all you have; exhaust yourself completely.

Fourth Stage: 15 minutes

STOP! Freeze wherever you are, in whatever position you find yourself. Don't arrange the body in any way. A cough, a movement, anything, will dissipate the energy flow and the effort will be lost. Be a witness to everything that is happening to you.

Fifth Stage: 15 minutes

Celebrate! With music and dance express whatsoever is there. Carry your aliveness with you throughout the day.

If your meditation space prevents you from making noise, you can do this silent alternative: rather than throwing out the sounds, let the catharsis in the second stage take place entirely through bodily movements. In the third stage, the sound Hoo! can be hammered silently inside, and the fifth stage can become an expressive dance.

- *From Osho.com*

A study published by Anuj Bansal, Ashish Mittal and Vikas Seth (2016) in Journal of Clinical and Diagnostic Research titled "Osho Dynamic Meditation's Effect on Serum Cortisol Level" found that significant reductions in plasma cortisol levels (stress marker) occurred when participants were tested after 21 days of dynamic meditation. The study concludes the following:

"This suggests that Osho dynamic meditation produces anti-stress effects. Accordingly, the dynamic meditation is an appropriate candidate for integrative stress management

options and related research. The mechanism of action of this meditation could, at least in part, be attributed to the release of repressed emotions such as crying which has already been documented to reduce the stress and stress hormone cortisol.

Therefore, it can be concluded that a regular practice of dynamic meditation could be recommended as a healing intervention for the amelioration of stress and stress related physical and mental disorders. More clinical studies should be done on dynamic meditation to prove its efficacy and become an approved therapy in hospitals."

A session of dynamic meditation lasts for one hour. I recommend at least 10-20 sessions of dynamic meditation in total. But you can do dynamic meditation everyday if you want to. You can get music for dynamic meditation from Osho.com and many other online resources.

Two Types of Meditation - Open Monitoring and Focused Attention

If you take any spiritual practice or meditation technique, it will fall under one of the two types of meditation: open monitoring and focused attention.

Focused attention meditation is any meditation which involves focusing your entire attention on an object of meditation. Focused attention meditation develops concentration and helps to achieve good mindfulness. Open monitoring involves being open and attentive to anything that happens in your consciousness every moment. Mindfulness and witnessing are examples of open monitoring meditations.

Buddha in the eightfold path lists 'Right mindfulness' as the seventh one and 'Right samadhi' as the last one. These two are actually the core of the spiritual path. Samadhi is a focused attention meditation and sammasati or right mindfulness is an open monitoring meditation. According to Buddha, Samadhi can improve mindfulness and mindfulness can improve samadhi. So, these two practices are complementary to each other.

Both of the types require you to allocate certain time for meditation, sit in a comfortable posture preferably with crossed legs and close your eyes. With focused attention, you will focus all your attention on one object. For example, you can choose the blue color of an empty sky as the object of meditation. You have to fix your attention solely on that one object and you have to keep bringing your attention to the object of your meditation whenever you find that your attention has wavered.

With mindfulness, an open monitoring meditation, you have to witness your breath, body sensations and thoughts as they arise every moment. Usually you are taught to first focus on breath and then extend your awareness to your thoughts and feelings. This meditation is nothing but witnessing practice done seated and with closed eyes.

All these seated meditation practices can be done regularly. But integrating witnessing into all activities of our daily life is more important and more practical for the people of modern times.

Focused Attention

For most people, the word meditation always means focused attention. Traditionally focused attention meditation is quite popular, even though open monitoring meditation is very important. Yogic process of dhyana and samadhi, upasana in Vedanta and Shamatha in Buddhism are some of the popular examples of focused attention meditation.

In the school of Yoga, there are eight limbs or steps. The last four limbs train you to achieve perfection in focused attention meditation. Those four limbs are Pratyahara, Dharana, Dhyana and Samadhi.

Pratyahara is the process of withdrawal of senses. Once you sit cross legged in a place where you won't be disturbed, the first step is to withdraw your attention from the outside world. Dharana is concentration or fixed attention. You can pick an object of meditation and focus your attention on the object while you keep your eyes closed. As soon as you find that your mind has wandered away, you simply have to bring it back to the object of meditation. It is important to not to feel bad, frustrated or guilty when your mind has wandered. It is quite normal and it will happen again and again in the beginning. You need to accept it as natural, stop fighting with your mind and keep bringing your attention back to the object of meditation as soon as you realize that your mind has wandered. Dhyana is the sustained attention towards the object of meditation.It is an unbroken stream of attention. Finally, Samadhi can be said as a complete absorption. It is the final stage of yoga.

Upasana meditations are mentioned in Upanishads but they are rarely practiced today. Instructions on how to do them are not very clear. It is a little bit different from yogic meditations. Upasana requires certain visualizations. They are also called as vidyas or brahmavidyas. There are about 32 vidyas mentioned in the upanishads.

Samadhi or shamatha in Buddhism is covered extensively in many Buddhist scriptures. They describe 8 different states of meditations or jhanas. Usually, all techniques of focused attention meditations result in extreme bliss or joy when the meditation attains perfection. It is very important to not to get attached to this temporary experiences of bliss. Focused attention meditations are practiced only as an aid to improve open monitoring meditations. There is nothing much to learn about this meditation. The term 'focused attention' explains it all.

Open Monitoring

Mindfulness is the open monitoring meditation in Buddhism. There are two types: formal mindfulness and informal mindfulness. Informal mindfulness is just another name for witnessing. In formal mindfulness, you sit cross legged, close your eyes and do the same witnessing practice. But they usually teach you to witness your breath first.

Mindfulness meditation was popularized in west by Jon Kabat-Zinn. Ever since it became popular, a lot of scientific studies have been conducted on it. Studies have shown that mindfulness improves wellbeing and reduces stress, depression and pain. It is also used in the treatment of drug addiction. It has been found the change the perception of self when practiced long term. Mindfulness is used in many therapies like Mindfulness-based stress reduction, Mindfulness-based cognitive therapy, Acceptance and commitment therapy, Dialectical behavior therapy, Mode deactivation therapy etc.

Here are the instructions for practicing mindfulness:

1. Find a place where there is solitude and silence. Make sure you won't be disturbed. Sit cross legged, keep your body and mind erect and close your eyes.
2. Keep your attention on your breathing. Observe and feel the sensations at the nostril when the breath moves in and moves out.
3. Pay attention to whether each breath is long or short.
4. If your attention wanders, simply return the attention to your breath.

5. Pay attention to moment to moment experience as they arise and pass away. Observe the body sensations and the movements of the thoughts with no judgments, with a sense of acceptance and curiosity.

Self-inquiry technique taught by Ramana Maharshi and Nididhyasana of Vedanta can also be classified under open monitoring practices. We will learn about nididhyasana in a different chapter. Self-inquiry is basically an inquiry into each thought that arises. In the book 'Nan Yar' (Who Am I), Ramana Maharshi describes self-inquiry as follows:

"When other thoughts arise, one should not pursue them, but should inquire: 'To whom do they arise?' It does not matter how many thoughts arise. As each thought arises, one should inquire with diligence, "To whom has this thought arisen?". The answer that would emerge would be "To me". Thereupon if one inquires "Who am I?", the mind will go back to its source; and the thought that arose will become quiescent. With repeated practice in this manner, the mind will develop the skill to stay in its source. When the mind that is subtle goes out through the brain and the sense organs, the gross names and forms appear; when it stays in the heart, the names and forms disappear. Not letting the mind go out, but retaining it in the Heart is what is called "inwardness" (antarmukha). Letting the mind go out of the Heart is known as "externalisation" (bahir-mukha). Thus, when the mind stays in the Heart, the 'I' which is the source

of all thoughts will go, and the Self which ever exists will
shine. Whatever one does, one should do without the egoity
"I". If one acts in that way, all will appear as of the nature of
Siva (God)."

Self-inquiry can be practiced anytime, no matter what you are doing.
It is similar to witnessing in this sense. Ramana Maharshi
recommended self-inquiry as the quickest and direct way to
liberation. I would suggest you to do all these different types of
practices as a supplementary to witnessing. But always consider
witnessing as the top priority and make sure you integrate it as much
as possible in your daily life.

Chapter Seven: Spiritual Crisis - The Dark Night of the Soul

In this chapter, we are going to discuss the dark side of the spiritual path. This is something that you need to be aware of. When you are walking on the spiritual path, you are dealing with the most important thing in your life which is your self concept. The identification with the image in your head doesn't want to go so easily. Your ego will resist the transformation. People may sometimes undergo a period of crisis because of this. In spiritual circles, this is popularly called as the dark night of the soul.

People may go through one or multiple phases of the dark night of the soul. It always happens because of some kind of resistance. Your ego may either want to pull you back to the older way of living or take credit for the spiritual progress and want you to get liberated very quickly. Because, ego wants to add 'liberation' as one of the accomplishments of this separate self, which will never happen. Dark night of the soul is a revenge made by ego in some form. Sometimes the effects of the dark night can be very serious and may require medical help. But most of the people who are aware of this usually get past this stage without much problems.

Dark night of the soul is a phase when your whole life seems to be meaningless. But the search for a meaning or purpose in life is actually an attempt to protect and enhance your self-concept. Self-concept always needs more meaning to thrive. But life doesn't really have a conceptual meaning or a purpose. As Osho said, life is not a problem to be solved but a mystery to be lived. We want meanings to enrich our self-concept; but absolute freedom comes when the self-concept is completely renounced and the identification with it is completely gone.

So, is life meaningless? It is more correct to say that search for meaning in life is meaningless. Because, the significance of life is not in its conceptual meaning that we want to assign to it, but the life itself. It has to be lived in its fullest, with full involvement.

Ego always searches for some meaning. It pushes you to collect some meanings and definitions of a fictitious entity that you carry in your head, which you think is 'you'. By assigning some attributes, goals and a story, you have defined yourself as a person separate from the whole existence. Awakening dawns when any search for meaning completely disappears.

Being as a spiritual seeker is like groping in the dark. You don't know completely about the destination yet and it seems uncertain and unknown. You can't go back to the old way of living either. You seem to be stuck in the path, feel alone and don't seem to fit in with the rest of the society. This is also one of the reasons for the dark night of the soul.

Spiritual Crisis and DSM-IV

The Diagnostic and Statistical Manual of Mental Disorders (DSM), published by the American Psychiatric Association (APA) contains the complete classification of mental disorders which is used by psychiatrists to diagnose their patients. Few decades before, the phases of the dark night were treated like any other mental disorder. But after the mid 1970s, psychiatrists and researchers began to recognize spiritual crisis for what it is. David Lukoff, Ph.D., is a Professor of Psychology at Saybrook Graduate School along with two psychiatrists (Francis Lu, MD and Robert Turner, MD) proposed a new diagnostic category in DSM-IV which was published in 1994. Spiritual crisis actually includes a wide variety of problems that arise in religious and spiritual life. The dark night of the soul can be said as one of the categories of spiritual crisis.

DSM-IV defines spiritual crisis as follows:

> "V62.89: This category can be used when the focus of clinical attention is a religious or spiritual problem. Examples include distressing experiences that involve loss or questioning of faith, problems associated with conversion to a new faith, or questioning of other spiritual values which may not necessarily be related to an organized church or religious institution. (American Psychiatric Association, 1994, p. 685)"

The problem that we are talking about as the dark night of the soul is categorized as 'Spiritual Emergency', a term coined by Dr.

Stanislav Grof M.D, a Czech psychiatrist, along with his wife Christina Grof.

Dr. Stanislav Grof said the following in an interview:

> "There exist spontaneous non-ordinary states that would in the west be seen and treated as psychosis, treated mostly by suppressive medication. But if we use the observations from the study of non-ordinary states, and also from other spiritual traditions, they should really be treated as crises of transformation, or crises of spiritual opening. Something that should really be supported rather than suppressed. If properly understood and properly supported, they are actually conducive to healing and transformation."

Bhakthi Yoga - The Path of Love

Since we are discussing dark night, I think this is the perfect time to introduce something called Bhakthi yoga - The Path of love. There have been people in the history, who were crazy devotees of God and showed unconditional love towards God. For them God is not just the ruler of the world who answers prayers or punishes evil doers, but He is actually the beloved, the one with whom the heart longs to unite with. Contrary to other paths and methods, a belief in a personal God becomes a prerequisite. What they call as the union with God is same as the liberation that we are talking about. Their quest for human liberation is like a love affair. They personify the absolute reality as God and long to unite with him. Let us call them Bhakthi yogis.

Something that needs to be remembered here: The path of love is not something anybody can just follow by following some instructions. Unless for some reason the love arises naturally, it is not the path of love. So, the purpose of this section is just to let you know that such a thing exists, not to give you a method or technique to follow. You cannot choose the path of love. It happens to some people for no reason. But still, Bhakthi, the devotion to God has been recommended by many liberated masters as a path. Personally, I don't think that devotion can be developed as any other skill. You can develop your ability to witness but you cannot develop love. Anyway, Bhakthi yoga deserves a mention in this book, because the book will be incomplete without talking about it.

Traditions like Christian mysticism seem to be a combination of love, Christian theology and certain practices that one can follow. But this tradition relies heavily on the Christian belief system, customs and terminology. It looks like a detailed path to liberation has been created in Christian mysticism based on the own experiences of these Bhakthi yogis. But one reason I think it will not work for people even if they try it is because, the love affair with divine is not something that can be acquired or developed by following a set of instructions.

Christian Mysticism offers a threefold path that involves Purification, Illumination and Unification. Purification is a phase during which one purifies his senses, mind and body by acts like prayer, fasting, charity etc and by following severe asceticism. Illumination is the phase where a person may see mystical visions and acquires insight about many things. Unification is the actual liberation where a person merges with divine and loses his psychological boundaries and duality. When I read the descriptions of this path, I understand that the only logic they used is 'This is what I did and this is what happened. So, if you follow these steps, you will be liberated too'. But a main difference between the actual Bhakthi yogis and people who imitate what Bhakthi yogis did is this: For Bhakthi yogis, the love with divine is natural. But people who follow the Bhakthi yogis and create a replica of the Bhakthi yogis life do not usually have the natural love with divine.

Now, let us look at the life of an actual Bhakthi Yogi. Ramakrishna Paramhamsa, the guru of Swami Vivekananda was essentially a Bhakthi yogi. He was crazy about God and was in a divine love affair. He also used to experience visions where he could directly talk with a physical form of God. Seeing visions and hearing voices are common for people who are in the path of Bhakthi. Such things are possible. The neural mechanisms which are at work during such visions are the same mechanisms which are behind the hallucinations experienced by someone suffering from schizophrenia. But the main difference between the psychosis experienced by a patient of schizophrenia and the psychosis experienced by Bhakthi yogi is that the latter is transformative and the results are positive.

The love affair of Bhakthi yogis was extraordinary. There were often viewed as insane by a few people in the society because of their unconventional ways. Let us look at a poem by Meerabai, who regarded Lord Krishna as her husband:

> *My Dark One has gone to an alien land.*
>
> *He has left me behind, he's never returned, he's never sent me a single word.*
>
> *So I've stripped off my ornaments, jewels and adornments, cut my hair from my head.*
>
> *And put on holy garments, all on his account, seeking him in all four directions.*
>
> *Mira: unless she meets the Dark One, her Lord, she doesn't even want to live.*

- *John Stratton Hawley (2002), Asceticism (Editors: Vincent Wimbush, Richard Valantasi), Oxford University Press, ISBN 978-0195151381, page 303*

'The dark one' in the poem means Lord Krishna. The poem reveals the pain of separation. This pain of separation from God is often poetically expressed by many Bhakthi yogis in their poems. For them, the agony of the separation was the greatest dark night of the soul.

The word 'Dark night' itself comes from a poem written by St. John of the Cross. He was a very popular Christian mystic. The poem

'Dark Night of the Soul' narrates the journey of a person to liberation through Bhakthi Yoga. The term 'Dark Night' is used to indicate that the destination, which is God, is unknowable.

Sufism, a mystic school of Islam is also a product of Bhakthi Yoga. Similar to Christian Mysticism, Sufism relies heavily on Islamic theology and belief system, even though the core of sufism is love. The Sufi word for Nirvana or Moksha is 'fitra', which is translated to English as 'primordial human nature'. They believe that Abraham and Mohammed were the perfect embodiments of fitra. The teachings are transmitted by a Guru to disciples. Sufis insist that a disciple should serve his Guru and live with him for a long period of time.

All these Bhakthi schools take the love towards God as the main theme, show more value to their own religion and beliefs and also seem to adopt methods from other schools about human liberation. The methods used in these traditions may be helpful but I don't recommend choosing a tradition like Sufism, Christian mysticism or Gaudiya Vaishnavism. These paths are mixed with a lot of beliefs and not quite empirical as Buddhism. When I read about various traditions around the world and go through their methods and teachings, I can clearly see that the way Buddha guided people was more practical and empirical.

The dark night phase that a seeker goes through can be compared to the the pain of separation that a Bhakthi Yogi goes through. A dark night or a spiritual crisis is actually a good indication for progress in the path. It is very important for the seeker to be courageous and use dark night as an opportunity for going deeper in witnessing and mindfulness.

One thing that I need to tell you about liberation is that a lot of things said about liberation and the methods to reach liberation are generalized conclusions that was made based upon observing a few individuals. Nobody had a streamlined method such as scientific method to test and verify the effectiveness of spiritual practices and the behavioral changes that occur after liberation. Usually, a person who was liberated always suggested the methods that worked for him when he provided guidance for other seekers. But when you develop methods or theories by generalizing things based on one person's personal journey, it is not always 100% reliable. Bridging science and spirituality is the best solution for this problem.

Chapter Eight: The History of Non-Dual Wisdom

Don't skip this chapter! You may not be a great fan of history but this chapter is included in this book for a reason. When you see how certain ideas evolved historically, it helps to understand many things and remove many misunderstandings. Once you have finished reading this chapter, you will have a better understanding of the spiritual path.

The Vedic Period

The religious, philosophical and spiritual history of India goes back to the period when Vedic hymns were composed. Vedic verses are dated back to 1700 BC and the total body of Vedic texts have been divided into four: Rig veda, Sama Veda, Yajur Veda and Atharvaveda. Many Indians revere these vedas as holy and believe that Vedas are eternal and infallible. Vedas have been considered as divine revelations, revealed to ancient seekers when they were in deep meditation.

The content of the Vedas are mainly about rituals done before the fire. All natural forces like fire, dawn, wind etc were worshipped in ancient India. The people had a custom of sacrificing their valuables in fire to please the vedic deities so that the deities would grant them material wealth and heaven. These sacrifices were done while priests were singing the appropriate hymns which were sung in a standardized way. Many people interpret Vedas in different ways. I have read some articles where the authors pick up certain vedic verses in random, trying to prove that they have some secret code which convey a lot of truth about the spiritual path. Many people try to fit some scientific theories to ambiguous Vedic verses, claiming that Vedas are full of scientific facts. They believe that many of the modern discoveries have already been made by Vedic poets.

But if one looks with an unbiased mind, it is not difficult to understand that Vedas are just a compilation of various text and hymns created by different people probably over a period of thousand years or more. Also, it is very easy to see that Vedas emphasize these fire rituals more than anything else. Since the language and prosody was probably a recent development for people in Vedic age, it is understandable that they had various sentiments regarding Vedic verses. They saw them as holy and they thought that those verses have to be preserved. Vedas have been transmitted by oral tradition from ancient days to till date. People have tried to preserve the accent and pronunciation of Vedic verses as much as possible, because of the holiness they have attributed to vedas.

One of the Vedic hymns clearly mentions that the hymn is being composed by the poet just like a craftsman makes a car.The fact that vedic hymns are just human composition is evident from the below verse:

"As a skilled craftsman makes a car, a singer I, Mighty One!
this hymn for thee have fashioned.
If thou, O Agni, God, accept it gladly, may we obtain
thereby the heavenly Waters.

- *Rig Veda - Mandala 5/Hymn 2.11; Translated by*
  Ralph Thomas Hotchkin Griffith; Source:
  wikisource.org"

People usually say that Vedas are 'apaurusheya', which means 'not of a man'. They are believed to be the breath of God. But each Vedic hymn is actually attributed to a particular sage, implying that each verse was written by the sage whose name is attributed to it. People who believe in the apaurusheya theory explain it by saying that these were divine revelations revealed to sages when they were in deep meditation. But in reality, Vedas, excluding Upanishads, hardly have any spiritual wisdom. If the divine has to reveal something to the human beings, I would expect a lot more than the information on how to conduct various vedic rituals. Vedantic tradition considers Vedas (mainly the Upanishads) as the only authority to truth and as infallible and eternal.

Let us look at a hymn in Atharva Veda:

"1. May Agni drive the takman away from here, may Soma,
the press-stone, and Varuna, of tried skill; may the altar, the
straw (upon the altar), and the brightly-flaming fagots (drive
him away)! Away to naught shall go the hateful powers!

2. Thou that makest all men sallow, inflarning them like a searing fire, even now, O takman, thou shalt become void of strength: do thou now go away down, aye, into the depths!

The takman that is spotted, covered Nvith spots, like reddish sediment, him thou, (O plant) of unremitting potency, drive away down below!

4. Having made obeisance to the takman, I cast him down below: let him, the champion of Sakambhara, return again to the Mahâvrishas!

5. His home is with the Mûgavants, his home with the Mahâvrishas. From the moment of thy birth thou art indigenous with the Balhikas.

6. O takman, vyâla, vîgada, vyânga, hold off (thy missile) far! Seek the gadabout slave-girl, strike her with thy bolt!

7. O takman, go to the Mûgavants, or to the Balhikas farther away! Seek the lecherous Sûdra female: her, O takman, give a good shaking-up!

8. Go away to the Mahâvrishas and the Mûgavants, thy kinsfolk, and consume them! Those (regions) do we bespeak for the takman, or these regions here other (than ours).

9. (If) in other regions thou dost not abide, mayest thou that art powerful take pity on us! Takman, now, has become eager: he will go to the Balhikas.

10. When thou, being cold, and then again deliriously hot, accompanied by cough, didst cause the (sufferer) to shake, then, O takman, thy missiles were terrible: from these surely exempt us!

11. By no means ally thyself with balâsa, cough and spasm! From there do thou not return hither again: that, O takman, do I ask of thee!

12. O takman, along with thy brother balâsa, along with thy sister cough, along with thy cousin pâman, go to yonder foreign folk!

13. Destroy the takman that returns on (each) third day, the one that intermits (each) third day, the one that continues without intermission, and the autumnal one; destroy the cold takman, the hot, him that comes in summer, and him that arrives in the rainy season!

14. To the Gandhâris, the Mâgavants, the Angas, and the Magadhas, we deliver over the takman, like a servant, like a treasure!

- *I.V,22, Hymns of Atharva Veda - Translated by M.Bloomfield & edited by F.Max Muller*

The hymn talks about a disease or a class of diseases called 'takman'. The hymn basically wants the takman to go away from their kingdom and instead affect the people in some other nearby kingdoms. The author of the hymn says that takman should leave their own country and affect the people including innocent women who live in the kingdoms like Gandharis, the Magavants, the Angas, the Magadhas etc. So it was obvious that these people hated the kingdoms like Magadha and Anga.

Why would the people want the cruel disease to go and affect the innocent people in these kingdoms? First of all, a text which is a divine revelation, which is infallible as well as eternal, will not have such an aversion to all the people living in a particular kingdom. Second, the reason why they didn't like these kingdoms was because these kingdoms had their own beliefs and philosophy which was not in agreement with Vedic thoughts. The people in those kingdoms didn't give much importance to Vedas and Vedic rituals. This was the reason for their hatred. The regions mentioned in the hymn belong to the kingdoms that were present in the northern and eastern part of Ancient India. Gandhari was located in the northernmost part of India whereas Anga and Magadha covered the regions of present day Bihar and the nearby regions.

Let us have a look at the map of Vedic India:

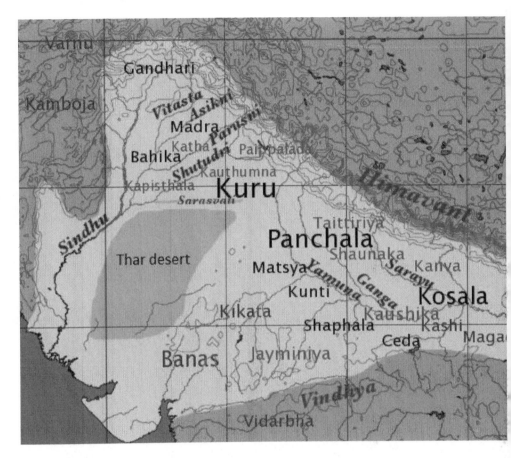

Do you see the kingdoms Magadha, Anga and Videha in the right side? These regions are very important. The people who lived in these regions should have been rebellious and critical thinkers. They didn't accept the authority of Vedas. Buddha, who rejected Vedas and Vedic rituals, lived much of his life in the kingdom of Magadha.

Rebellion Against Vedas

The period between 900 BC and 600 BC is probably the golden period of spirituality. This is when the two oldest and major Upanishads namely Brihadaranyaka Upanishad and Chandogya Upanishad were compiled. These two Upanishads were also anthologies of different poems composed by different people. But a sage who is mentioned in these Upanishad is Yajnavalkya, who was from Videha kingdom that is right next to Magadha. Brihadaranyaka Upanishad itself is credited to Yajnavalkya but scholars believe that the text was edited and interpolated over a period of time. It is important to note that the region where Yajnavalkya lived was full of those rebellious people who were against the authority of Vedas. Yajnavalkya and Uddalaka Aruni are considered as the earliest proponents of non-dual wisdom.

Western scholars who studied Upanishads conclude that they are the results of the protests of kings against the influence of Vedic rituals and the priests who conducted them.

Swami Nikhilananda, in his book 'The Principal Upanishads' writes the following:

> *"Therefore several Western writers have contended that the Upanishads represent a protest of the kshatriyas against the influence of the brahmins." They contend also that the Knowledge of Atman, whatever its origin, was cultivated primarily by the kshatriyas and accepted by the brahmins only later on. Hindu scholars, however, do not accept this view."*

- *'The Principal Upanishads' by Swami Nikhilananda*

However, I see that Hindu scholars are extremely biased in this matter. Because, Hindus have always seen Upanishads as complementary to Vedas and not against them. In fact, most of the Hindus consider Upanishads as part of Vedas. All traditional Vedantins regard Upanishads as a part of Vedas and they also believe that Vedas and Upanishads are eternal and infallible. I have read both sides of the arguments but I can see very clearly that most of the poems in Upanishads were indeed a protest against Vedas.

But the composers of Upanishads conveyed what they wanted to convey with metaphors and analogies. They used the terminology of Vedas probably to avoid the problems that arise because of connotation, which we discussed in an earlier chapter. If they had protested Vedas directly and openly, these Upanishads might not have survived the test of time. People could never accept anything that went against Vedas.

Also, I won't put all verses of Upanishads in one category and all verses of Vedas into another. There are verses in Upanishads which seem to be supporting Vedas too. But we always need to remember that when we read an Upanishad, we are reading an anthology of various poems which reflect the thoughts of the individual composers.

It was during this period, that Sramana movement arose in the country. A sramana was an individual wandering monk, free from traditions, who practiced severe austerities in the pursuit of liberation. Also, it was during this period that Buddhism was born and Jainism also flourished.

Buddha was probably unaware of the recently composed Upanishads. Atharva veda was probably not a part of the sacred Vedic canon either. It must have been an independent collection of texts. But since Buddha himself was searching for a way to liberation and since he also went to a lot of gurus, we can assume that nondual wisdom was already born and the ways to attain it had already been somewhat established before Buddha was born. People who were liberated and who were guiding others for liberation should have existed as independent gurus who did or didn't associate themselves with any tradition.

But before Buddha, no one approached the path to liberation in such an empirical way. The earliest texts which talk about liberation seem to advocate practicing severe austerities including self-mortification. They not only emphasized renunciation but also promoted the idea that one should torture himself to attain liberation. Buddha, probably for the first time in history, advocated the middle way, the way of moderation between the extremes of sensual indulgence and self-mortification.

All schools of thought which didn't accept Vedas as authority were named as 'nastika' schools. Buddhism and Jainism were the largest of all nastika schools. Schools which accepted the authority of Vedas were categorized as 'Astika' schools. Samkhya, the oldest astika school of Indian thought emerged as a distinct school during 5th century BCE, which put together many independent ideas into a single system. But, Samkhya didn't consider Vedas as the only authority to the truth, even though it accepted Vedas as important.

An Overview of Samkhya

Richard Garbe, a German Indologist, stated in the following:

> *"The origin of the Sankhya system appears in the proper light only when we understand that in those regions of India which were little influenced by Brahmanism the first attempt had been made to solve the riddles of the world and of our existence merely by means of reason. For the Sankhya philosophy is, in its essence, not only atheistic but also inimical to the Veda."*

> - *Richard Garbe (1892). Aniruddha's Commentary and the original parts of Vedantin Mahadeva's commentary on the Sankhya Sutras Translated, with an introduction to the age and origin of the Sankhya system. pp. xx–xxi.*

As he says, the ideas towards liberation, including the ones found in Buddhism and Samkhya emerged in the regions of India which were little influenced by the Vedic tradition. Samkhya school existed long before Yoga and Vedanta emerged as independent schools of thought.

Samkhyakarika of Isvarakrsna is the earliest surviving authoritative text of Samkhya school. The first sutra of Samkhyakarika starts very meaningfully, similar to the four noble truths of Buddhism. The first sutra is explained as follows:

> "From the torment caused by the three kinds of pain, proceeds a desire for inquiry into the means of terminating them; if it be said that (the inquiry) is superfluous since visible means exist, (we reply), not so; because (in the visible means) there is the absence of certainty (in the case of the means) and permanency (of pain).

> - Samkhyakarika of Isvarakrsna - Translated by Swami Virupakshananda, Sri Ramakrishna Math"

The sutra says that because of human suffering, there is an inquiry into the means of cessation of suffering. But then the question arises: There is always visible means to end suffering, like indulging in pleasure and accumulating wealth etc. When such visible means of ending the suffering available, what is the need for the inquiry? The sutra also replies to the question saying that all these visible means are not guaranteed to remove suffering. The suffering always returns and not permanently removed.

Then the second question arises. When Vedas promise wealth in this life and heaven in afterlife, why shouldn't people rely on Vedas instead of doing an inquiry to end suffering? The second sutra replies to this objection:

> "The scriptural means is like the obvious means since it is linked with impurity, decay and excess. The means contrary

to both and proceeding from the Discriminative Knowledge
of the Manifest, the Unmanifest and the Spirit, is superior.

- *Sutra II, Samkhyakarika of Isvarakrsna - Translated by*
  Swami Virupakshananda, Sri Ramakrishna Math

The detailed commentary that comes after this explains the sutra. This sutra clearly indicates that by all means, Sankhya didn't advocate the ritualistic life prescribed in Vedas as a means to end human suffering. It says that since Vedic rituals involve animal slaughter which is impure and since the results lack permanency, the discrimination between the observer and the observed, the subject and the object is the preferable means to end suffering.

The commentary then explains everything in detail and finally gives the following summary:

"The literal meaning of the words of the Karika is this: The
means of destroying pain in the form of immediate
Discriminative Knowledge of the Spirit as different from
Matter, is contrary to the Vedic means that are capable of
removing pain, and hence it is preferable. The Vedic means
also are good inasmuch as they are prescribed by the Veda
and as such capable of alleviating pain to a certain extent.
The Discriminative Knowledge of the Spirit as distinct from
Matter is also good; of these two excellent means, the
Discriminative Knowledge of the Spirit that is quite distinct
from Matter, is superior.

- *Sutra II, Samkhyakarika of Isvarakrsna - Translated by Swami Virupakshananda, Sri Ramakrishna Math"*

Here, the discriminative knowledge of spirit and matter is nothing but the discrimination of subject vs object that we discussed in the beginning. It is very clear that the oldest philosophical school of India suggests this discrimination as the first step towards the cessation of suffering.

Let me talk about a big misunderstanding before I continue. Usually, scholars regard Advaita as non-dual philosophy whereas samkhya and yoga as dual philosophies. They say this because while Advaita says that everything is one and not two, Samkhya says that there are multiple purushas (subjects). But actually, the final goal that Samkhya, Yoga and Advaita vedanta are talking about is the complete non-dual experience of reality. Once you are liberated, you experience the reality without even a slightest sense that you are separate from the existence. In your experience, there will be essentially no multiplicity, even though multiplicity will seem to exist in the sense perception. There will be no feeling that there is an other or another, after liberation. But even though this is experientially true, we still know by inference that each person has his own independent field of consciousness. It is only based on this inference, Samkhya and Yoga say that there are multiple purushas. But when it comes to the nature of liberation that they are talking about, Samkhya, Yoga and Vedanta point to one nondual wisdom.

Also, discriminating between the subject and the object doesn't mean that we are splitting the reality. The discrimination is only done to remove the veil of separation. After years and years of practicing witnessing with a proper and clear discrimination of the subject and the object, the observer and the observed merge together in our experience.

The Emergence of Yoga

Yoga is very popular in the West as a physical exercise. But Yoga is actually much more than that. It is one of the six schools of thought in India, just like Samkhya and Vedanta. Yoga is a school that guides people to end their suffering and attain liberation.

Yoga also stresses the importance of the discrimination of the subject and the objects. Sutra 2.26 of Patanjali Yoga sutras says 'viveka khyAti aviplava hana upayah' which means 'uninterrupted discriminative view is the means to liberation and the cessation of suffering.' As we already saw, the word 'viveka' means the discrimination of the subject and the objects.

Yoga came from Sankhya. They are essentially the same except one important concept. Samkhya doesn't talk about a personal God and doesn't consider it as necessary. But Yoga brings in the concept of Ishwara, who is a special Purusha. In Patanjali Yoga sutras, there are a few sutras which talk about Ishwara and define him as a special purusha or a special subject.

In the modern times, most of the people have never heard of Samkhya. The reason is obvious. Any school of thought which rejected or ignored the concept of a personal God did not survive and flourish in India. Because, people simply could not accept that God didn't exist.

Yoga describes the final destination as nirvikalpa samadhi. Literally, nirvikalpa means 'without alternative'. But in this word it means the loss of distinctions and the merger of knower, knowledge and the known. A liberated person's experience of reality is always without distinctions; it is always nirvikalpa.

But many people use the word 'nirvikalpa samadhi' to mean a temporary trance like state with a merger of the knower, known and knowledge, accompanied by a complete loss of body consciousness. There are anecdotes which talk about people immersed in nirvikalpa samadhi, with no body consciousness, movement ,food and water for many days.

Traditional vedanta doesn't talk about these trance-like states of bliss and it doesn't consider these trances as necessary. Not everyone who gets liberated goes into such samadhis either. But the reality of liberated people is indeed nirvikalpa anyway, as they don't feel the distinctions of 'me' vs 'world' or 'me' vs 'other'. In order to distinguish this natural experience of nirvikalpa while fully functioning in the world from those trance like states, the word sahaja samadhi is used. When a person is liberated but fully functioning in the world like others, he is in sahaja samadhi.

The School of Vedanta

After the composition of the 13 principal Upanishads, sometime down the line Upanishads also became a part of Vedas. Then, the whole Vedas got divided into two sections : Karma Kanda and Jnana Kanda.

The word Karma means action. But usually the word Karma in the everyday usage was a term to indicate the vedic rituals. Here, the word Karma was actually used to mean the essential duties. Failing to do vedic rituals was considered as a sin. Jnana means knowledge. Upanishads were a part of Jnana kanda. Jnana Kanda is used to transmit the spiritual wisdom and also to establish that Jnana is superior to karma. In post vedic times, people talked about two ways of living or two paths: The path of karma and the path of jnana. I will talk more about it in a moment.

Upanishads are included at the end of each Vedas. Because of this, the word Vedanta, which literally means 'end of Vedas', was always used to mean Upanishads. Before Vedanta was established as a separate school, the word Vedanta was just used to refer to Upanishads.

Some time between 450 BCE and 200 CE, Brahma Sutras, an important text in the school of Vedanta was composed. Brahmasutras attempts to establish the essence and the theme of Upanishads. It also logically refutes the views of other schools like Samkhya, Yoga and Buddhism. It takes the premise that Upanishads are infallible authority of the truth and uses the verses in Upanishads to disprove some theories of other schools. For example, the first part of Brahmasutras focuses on proving that the world originated from Brahman and refutes the view of the Samkhya school which says that the world originated from unconscious principle, pradhana.

But the only proof that Vedantic texts and commentaries offer for their view that Brahman is the cause of the Universe is the verses of Upanishads themselves. If Upanishads say something, then it must be true. There is no way to test this theory in anyway. But as I mentioned earlier, all these metaphysical theories about the creation of the world are totally unimportant for a spiritual path. The disagreement between Samkhya and Vedanta regarding the cause of creation touches on an important problem : The hard problem of consciousness. How can a conscious experience arise from matter?

Vedanta say that it is impossible for consciousness and cognition to arise from something that is not consciousness. Therefore, consciousness is the root cause of creation. But this is just a logical conclusion. Samkhya on the other hand says that Purusha is pure consciousness which doesn't do anything. Something that doesn't have attributes or function cannot engage in activity. Therefore, consciousness could not have created matter. Instead, world was just created from unconscious principle and purushas are just eternal fields of consciousness. Purusha is neither produced nor does it produce. This creation theory of samkhya is just a logical conclusion too.

Here, it is important to understand that both these are just theories. Both spirituality and science really don't have a clear, verifiable answer for the hard problem of consciousness. The only mistake people do is to sound certain and consider a possibility as certainty. Instead, we have to honestly agree that we don't know yet. Only a scientific research on the hard problem of consciousness can answer these questions. There is a deep mystery in the existence which seem to be something that cannot be answered.

Upanishads, Brahmasutras and Bhagwad Gita are the three important texts in Vedanta. They are collectively known as Prasthanatrayi. All these texts were open for multiple interpretations and they led to thousands of commentaries. Many of the famous commentaries led to 6 sub-schools of Vedanta. When I use the word Vedanta in this book, I am referring to Advaita Vedanta in specific.

Usually, a person who had written commentaries on the principal Upanishads, Brahmasutras and Bhagwad Gita was called as an Acharya. There have been many such acharyas in India. The most important one among them was Adi Shankara (788–820). He not only wrote commentaries on Prasthanatrayi but he also debated with a lot of scholars all over India in order to prove that Advaita Vedanta was correct and it is in accordance with Upanishads. Shankara is recognized as a liberated person by most of the religious and spiritual teachers.

Vedanta tradition considers Shankara as the most authoritative person in the history. They consider Shankara's interpretation of

Upanishads as the most reliable one. But we really need to question the premise that Shankara has for many of his arguments. The premise is something that we already discussed: Upanishads and Vedas are eternal and infallible. Is it true?

Let us have a look at a part of Shankara's commentary on Brihadaranyaka upanishad. The following excerpt includes the translation of some of the actual verses from the upanishad and Shankara's commentary on them:

> Verse 6: If man sees his reflection in water, he should recite the following Mantra : ' (May the gods grant) me lustre, manhood, reputation, wealth and merits.' She (his wife) is indeed the goddess of beauty among women. Therefore he should approach this handsome woman and speak to her.
>
> Shankara's commentary:
>
> If perchance he sees his reflection in water, he should recite the following Mantra : '(May the gods grant) me lustre,' etc. She is indeed the goddess of beauty among women. Therefore he should approach this handsome woman and speak to her, when she has taken a bath after three 'nights.
>
> Verse 7 : If she is not willing, he should buy her over; and if she is still unyielding, he should strike her with a stick or with the hand and proceed, uttering the following Mantra, 'I take   away your reputation,' etc. She is then actually discredited.

Shankara's commentary:

If she is not willing, he should buy her over, press his wishes through ornaments etc.; and if she is still unyielding, he should strike her with a stick or with the hand, and announcing that he was going to curse her and make her unfortunate, he should proceed,uttering the following Mantra : 'I take away your reputation: etc. As a result of that curse, she comes to be known as barren and unfortunate, and is then actually discredited.

- Shankara, Brihadaranyaka upanishad Bhasya - Chapter 6, section 4

The above verses show how totally male dominative the society was those days.. This example shows how one should not take everything just because it comes from a scripture or a person who is regarded as an authority. And I don't think that such infallible and eternal upanishads can advise someone to beat his wife if she doesn't agree for sex. People may say that these were later interpolations. But if that is the case, how could we trust Upanishads in the first place? Doesn't this question the authority of Upanishads?

Upanishads are poetry. All those verses were composed by independent poets and not all of them were necessarily liberated. We really can't be quite certain about those authors. Upanishads not only contain some extraordinary wisdom but they sometimes also contain absurd theories. Many of the things said in Upanishads should be taken metaphorically and not literally. Upanishads are full of eulogies and exaggeration, something that is natural to any poetry.

Let us look at how Upanishads describe what happens after death:

1. A person who neglects vedic rituals will go to hell and then take birth as an animal or a person in lower caste.

2. A person who performs all the prescribed vedic duties and rituals properly will go to the moon and rejoices with the deities who are living in the moon until the time allotted for his stay in the heaven is over. Then his soul comes down to earth through rain and it enters the plants via their roots. When somebody eats a fruit or vegetable from the plant which contains the soul, the soul becomes a part of his semen and gets passed on to a female after the intercourse. This is how people are reborn.

3. If a person practices Vedic rituals with an attitude of Karma Yoga or if the person practices devotion to a personal deity, he will attain a particular type of liberation called 'Krama Mukthi'. He will reach the world of Brahman after his death, stay there until the end of the world and finally merge with Brahman.

4. But if a person goes through Vedantic practices properly, he will get liberated while living on the earth and merge with Brahman instantly.

This sounds too fairy talish to me. No modern Vedanta teacher talks about these things because many of them never read Upanishads or

Shankara's commentaries on Upanishads directly. They simply pass on the knowledge that they got from their own gurus. But they claim that they teach according to the tradition. No one can really teach according to the tradition because scriptures actually contain things that many people of modern times would never consider as ethical or reasonable. They can't let go of tradition either, because the specialty of a Vedanta teacher lies in his lineage and how accurately they present the traditionally held ideas from the authoritative sources. Many students of traditional Vedanta don't realize that their attachment to tradition and obsession over studying and discussing scriptures are actually the traps which are stopping them from liberation.

I sometimes feel that Vedanta school actually had to compromise with Vedic tradition for its survival. It couldn't protest against Vedas openly because they thought that the school can't survive for long if it goes against Vedas. So they might have chosen to publicly endorse Vedas, made Upanishads as a part of Vedas and used Vedic terminology to convey the truth. Probably they did this all intentionally to avoid problems. Since they knew that Vedas and Upanishads are open to different ways of interpretation, they might have used their logical skills to interpret Upanishads and Vedas in a way that suits their philosophy. I am not being certain about it but I just see it as a possibility. Many liberated people have intentionally lied about certain things for good reasons.

Even though Vedanta school considers Vedas as authoritative, they emphasize Jnana over Karma. Vedantic texts repeatedly assert that inquiry into the cessation of suffering is far superior than performing vedic rituals. They also insist that sannyas (renunciation) is a must. A person who decides to take the path of jnana and get liberated should renounce all his properties and live his life by begging. And as per the established rules, only such a sannyasi can stop doing vedic rituals without incurring any sin.

Bhagwad Gita talks about two paths - Devotion to Karma and Devotion to knowledge (karmanistha and jnananishtha).. The one who practices karmanishtha is a karmayogi, who does all his vedic rituals while dedicating the fruits of action to a personal God. He does his actions with an attitude 'I am not the doer, I am an instrument in the hands of God'. He should follow this lifestyle until he is ready to take sannyas and renounce the world. Shankara talks about some rare exceptions like Janaka, who got liberated without taking Sannyas, but he clearly states in his commentaries that without sannyas liberation in this life is not possible. Karma yogis who don't progress to renounce the world will only attain Krama mukthi, according to Shankara.

But Shankara doesn't stop with this. He also says that people who are Brahmin by birth (Brahmins belong to the highest of four varnas) are the only people who can take sannyas. Some people claim that Varna system defines a Brahmin not based on his birth but based on his virtues. While this may be true to some extent and probably was true in a specific period of time in the history, at least in Shankara's opinion a Brahmin is a person who is born to Brahmin parents. This is very evident in his commentaries. So, if sannyas is required for liberation and if Brahmins are the only people who can take Sannyas, then why are all these traditional vedantic teachers say that everyone can become liberated? Well, they can't really teach what Shankara taught because a lot of Shankara's ideas will be totally unacceptable to people of the present time. How can human liberation be reserved to just one caste?

This is the problem if we stick to a tradition or rely on the authority of scriptures. Our world keeps changing. Even spiritual paths need to evolve to make sure that it is suitable for modern people. Renouncing the world is not really practical for people who live in this century. But the good news is, liberation is possible without renunciation, without having to give up all the possessions. Instead of sticking to the past, we can take advantage of the immense wisdom that Vedanta and Buddhism collectively offers, take out the essence of both the traditions by distinguishing the facts from the myths, bridge it with science and create a more practical and scientific path to liberation.

Chapter Nine: Vedanta and its Method of Teaching

Since you have a basic understanding about the spiritual path now, we will see how Vedanta guides a disciple towards liberation with its unique methodology of teaching. Before anyone begins to engage in a serious spiritual practice, Vedanta expects him to have developed certain qualifications. One should be ready as a disciple before he can get further guidance from a guru. But the truth is, developing those qualifications is the actual spiritual practice. Vedanta says that once you are completely ready as a disciple, you can get liberated even if the truth is pointed out to you once. This is said to put emphasis on the development of the qualifications and let you know that the major part of your spiritual journey is actually in developing those qualifications.

There is a paradox in the spiritual path. You cannot really do anything to get liberated. The reason is, liberation itself is the process of destroying the idea and the feeling that 'You are the doer'. It is not really a journey even though I use that word. Because any journey to get somewhere else only applies if you are not already there; any effort to achieve anything only applies if that is not already achieved. But when it comes to spirituality, the true self, the subject is already liberated and already there. The real you, the real self is the pure subject or the witness. Any action to reach anywhere or achieve anything is only done for achieving some kind of fulfillment; But the lack of fulfillment itself is caused by the idea and the feeling that you are a 'person', you are what you think you are and that you are separate from the existence. Liberation is neither an achievement nor the result of any actions, even though it may seem to be so in the beginning.

So, what exactly are we doing here in the name of spiritual practice? We are working to just remove the obstacles. Once the obstacles and the hardwired wrong notion of separation is removed, what is left or what is already there shines without any veil. The fourfold qualifications actually give you an idea on what needs to be worked on and developed.

A progress or an achievement is always a food for the little self (with lower case 's'); When you are worried about progress in anything, you can be sure that it is the ego which is checking if the standards are met. 'Am I progressing' is like asking 'am I becoming good enough now and meeting the standards of my ideal self?". But the path to liberation itself is a way to end this quest for fulfillment and the crave for becoming. So isn't it paradoxical to talk about a progress in the spiritual path? Should we probably call it as regressing instead of progressing? But it is not accurate either, because regressing implies that we are going back to a less developed state. I am still going to be using the word 'progress', but I am just reminding you of this paradox and once again trying to make you understand what exactly is happening in the spiritual practice.

Anyway, the real and easy way to check how much you have actually progressed in the spiritual path is to check how much you have developed these fourfold qualifications. When you practice mindfulness and witnessing, these fourfold qualifications will naturally develop. Let us look at the fourfold qualifications in detail now.

Fourfold Qualifications (Sadhana Chatushtaya)

Discrimination (Viveka)

This is the first and fundamental qualification that needs to be developed. I have already stressed the importance of the discrimination of subject and object throughout this book. Discrimination improves your ability to witness and witnessing further improves your ability to discriminate. So, the best way to improve it is to do witnessing more and more. Read the chapter on the subject and object as often as you want to get a clear understanding of discrimination.

Non-attachment (Vairagya)

We already saw how clinging to the objects or aggregates cause us suffering. Mistaking something that is not you as you is what we call as identification. As you become less identified with things, as you stop deriving your sense of self from what you have, what you know, what you have done and experienced, you automatically develop non-attachment. Again, witnessing helps you to gradually dis-identify and develop non-attachment.

There is a saying in India. They say that liberated people live their lives like the water droplets on a lotus leaf. Even though there is water on the lotus leaf, it doesn't really stick to the leaf. The lotus leaf doesn't become wet. Similarly, even though a liberated person engages in activities and worldly life with full involvement, he is completely detached. Nothing sticks to his mind! This is complete non-attachment.

The Six virtues

When you go deep in witnessing, it develops six virtues, which are together listed as one of the four qualifications. Here are those six virtues:

1. Tranquility (shama) - Control of your mind
2. Control of the senses (dama) - You are not to achieve this by forcing yourself, but it will automatically improve as the result of witnessing.
3. Self-withdrawal (Uparati) - You naturally withdraw from many activities which were motivated by craving. External objects lose your ability to control your mind;
4. Forbearance (titiksha) - Bearing with indifference all opposites such as pleasure and pain.
5. Faith (shraddha) - You need faith that the spiritual practices will actually work. You develop this trust in the spiritual practice as you start seeing the results.

6. Focus (samadhana) - Your mind becomes completely focused. Your ability to pay attention and peace of mind increases.

You are not going to work on these six virtues directly. As you do witnessing, mindfulness and other practices, they develop on their own accord. But this list is actually a quick way to check what has changed after a long term spiritual practice. Don't worry about these virtues too much and don't make them a part of your ideal self. If you are feeling that you are not good enough because these virtues have not developed to your satisfaction, then you are again reinforcing the idea of a separate self. You need to watch these tendencies of the mind as you witness your thoughts.

The Desire for Liberation (Mumukshutva)

As we saw in the first chapter, craving is the cause of suffering. But we can't stop craving directly. As you engage more and more in spiritual practice, your craving for multiple things get focused and becomes a deep longing for liberation. This motivates you to act on what needs to be done in the spiritual practice. At one point, your whole energy will get directed towards what needs to be done.

Basic Theory in Vedanta

Vedanta first talks about Brahman. According to Vedanta, Brahman is the cosmic principle. It doesn't have any attributes at all but it is the essence of everything. Vedanta says that Brahman is the material cause and efficient cause of all that exists. And, it cannot be described by words.

Here is how Upanishads define Brahman:

> "It is this Akshara (the Imperishable), O Gargi, so the knowers of Brahman say. It is neither gross nor subtle, neither short nor long, not red, not viscid, not shadowy, not dark, not the air, not the ether, not adhesive, tasteless, odourless, without the sense of sight, without the sense of hearing, without the vital principle, mouthless, without measure, neither interior nor exterior,. It eats nothing, nobody eats it."
>
> – Brihadaranyaka Upanishad 3-8-8

Buddha talks about nirvana in the same style:

> "There is that dimension, monks, where there is neither earth, nor water, nor fire, nor wind; neither dimension of the infinitude of space, nor dimension of the infinitude of consciousness, nor dimension of nothingness, nor dimension of neither perception nor non-perception; neither this world, nor the next world, nor sun, nor moon. And there, I say, there is neither coming, nor going, nor staying; neither passing away nor arising: unestablished, unevolving, without support [mental object]. This, just this, is the end of stress.
>
> • "Nibbāna Sutta: Unbinding (1)" (Ud 8.1), translated from the Pali by Thanissaro Bhikkhu. Access to Insight (BCBS

Edition), 3 September 2012,
http://www.accesstoinsight.org/tipitaka/kn/ud/ud.8.01.th
an.html ."

The idea presented here is that Brahman cannot be expressed by words and it doesn't have any attributes at all. Note that Buddha didn't use the word Brahman. In Buddhism, there is a word called dhammakaya, which literally means 'truth body'. The meaning of this word 'dhammakaya' is exactly the same as Brahman. Buddha didn't talk much about the subject or the observer self, because it cannot be talked about.

Brahman is considered as eternal and unborn:

> *Verily, that great unborn soul, undecaying, undying,*
> *immortal, fearless is Brahman*
>
> —   *Brihadaranyaka Upanishad 4.4.25*

Buddha also talked about this 'unborn' nature:

> *There is, monks, an unborn — unbecome — unmade —*
> *unfabricated. If there were not that unborn — unbecome —*
> *unmade — unfabricated, there would not be the case that*
> *escape from the born — become — made — fabricated*
> *would be discerned. But precisely because there is an unborn*
> *— unbecome — unmade — unfabricated, escape from the*
> *born — become — made — fabricated is discerned*
>
> *"Nibbāna Sutta: Unbinding (3)" (Ud 8.3), translated from the Pali*
> *by Thanissaro Bhikkhu. Access to Insight (BCBS Edition), 3*

September 2012,

http://www.accesstoinsight.org/tipitaka/kn/ud/ud.8.03.than.html .

After talking about Brahman, Vedanta says that you are that. The statement 'Tat tvam asi' (you are that) is found in Chandogya Upanishad for the first time, which then became a very popular statement in Vedanta. Note that Vedanta doesn't directly say you are the essence of existence. It first says that Brahman is the essence of existence and then says that you are that. Why is there a need for making two statements?

Brahman is a very important word in Vedas. In the earliest stage, the word Brahman was used to refer to the power of the words, sound and verses of Vedas. People believed that the sound of Vedic mantras had enormous power. Brahman had a very positive connotation in Vedic period. So nobody would accept the non-existence of Brahman. Recollect what we talked about in the chapter regarding the problem with words and you will understand what I mean. So, the composers of the hymns of Upanishads probably gave a new meaning to Brahman instead of denying that it didn't exist.

The concept of superimposition (adhyasa) is the core of Vedanta. It says that the reason for our suffering is ignorance (avidya) which happens because of superimposition. What is superimposition? You superimpose what is not you on you. Superimposing what is not Self on Self is ignorance. You mistake different things for Self when you are not any of them.

A classic example that is given in Vedanta is mistaking a rope for a snake in a dark night. When you see a rope in the dark and think it is a snake, you are immediately in panic and your body starts to tremble because of fear. But there is really no snake at all. You have superimposed the image of a snake on a rope. Once you realize that it is not a snake, your fear is gone. The same way, you have taken everything that is impermanent and superimposed them on you.

Before we continue, let us talk about the term 'atmajnana' (Self-knowledge) and understand what it means. The word 'atmajnana' literally means Self-knowledge. Vedanta says that only when you gain self-knowledge, you are liberated. But Self-knowledge is a misnomer, it was only used metaphorically. But this has caused a lot of misunderstanding. So, let me clear up this misunderstanding first.

Self, the subject, is not an object of knowledge. You cannot know the Self because you are it. The observer cannot be an object of knowledge. Self is the knower himself. So, the word self-knowledge doesn't mean that there is a special kind of knowledge about the world which is acquired after liberation. Self-knowledge is a term given to the removal of the superimposition. Once you experientially realize that you are not separate from existence, once you no longer consider yourself as a body or mind, you have got Self-knowledge.

But people misunderstand this. Many people today talk about knowing the truth without realizing what that truth is going to be. The truth is nothing but recognizing our false ideas as false ideas. You don't get informed about anything new. The removal of superimposition is known as the realization of truth. I mention this as a misunderstanding because I came across some people taking some pride in saying, 'I am not in the spiritual path to end my suffering or to feel good. I want to know the truth, That is why I am practicing meditation'. If you have had similar thoughts, then let me tell you once and for all: Liberation is all about ending the suffering. Suffering is the reason why people want to get liberated in the first place. Other than that, there is no mystical, magical, one-of-a kind or bizarre truth that you will find out after liberation.

The whole spiritual practice is about observing and then keep negating that you are not what that is observed. You keep discarding everything that arises and passes away as 'not this, not this'. This is called 'neti neti' in Vedanta. (The word 'Neti' can be split as 'na iti': which means : 'not!', thus... It explains the procedure of how you go about it).

Now, we need to ask a question. If Brahman is something which doesn't have any attributes, why does Vedanta sometimes define it with a lot of attributes and actions? The one that observes cannot have any attributes because all attributes can be observed, sensed or noticed or thought about in someway.

There is a reason for it. Because Vedanta has a unique and smart technique called 'Adhyaropa apavada'...

In order to discriminate between the subject and the object, Vedanta thinks that you need at least some conceptual basis to understand the subject. But the subject can never be conceptualized. In order to resolve this issue, Vedanta intentionally superimposes some attributes to this absolute truth of who you are. Remember, this is a deliberate and intentional superimposition done for the convenience. But at the final stage, Vedanta also negates these intentionally superimposed attributes. This method of intentional superimposition and negation is called as Adhyaropa Apavada.

This concept is well-explained in the following excerpt from Shankara's commentary on Brihadaranyaka Upanishad:

> "Who so knows the Self, thus described, as the fearless Absolute (brahman), himself becomes the Absolute, beyond fear. This is a brief statement of the meaning of the entire Upanishad. And in order to convey this meaning rightly, the fanciful alternatives of production, maintenance and withdrawal, and the false notion of action, its factors and results, are deliberately attributed to the Self as a first step. And then later the final metaphysical truth is inculcated by negating these characteristics through a comprehensive denial of all particular superimpositions on the Absolute, expressed in the phrase 'neither this nor that'.
>
> Just as a man, wishing to explain numbers from one to a hundred thousand billion (points to figures that he has drawn and) says, 'This figure is one, this figure is ten, this figure is a hundred, this figure is a thousand', and all the time his only purpose is to explain numbers, and not to affirm that the figures are numbers; or just as one wishing to

*explain the sounds of speech as repre sented by the written
letters of the alphabet resorts to a device in the form of a
palm-leaf on which he makes incisions which he later fills
with ink to form letters, and all the while, (even though he
point to a letter and say "This is the sound "so and so"") his
only purpose is to explain the nature of the sounds referred
to by each letter, and not to affirm that the leaf, incisions
and ink are sounds; in just the same way, the one real
metaphysical principle, the Absolute, is taught by resort to
many devices, such as attributing to it production (of the
world) and other powers. And then after wards the nature of
the Absolute is restated, through the concluding formula
'neither this nor that', so as to purify it of all particular
notions accruing to it from the various devices used to
explain its nature in the first place'.*

– Brihadaranyaka Bhasya IV.iv.25 – by Shankara

This unique teaching method called Adhyaropa Apavada is not
known and understood by a lot of long term students of Vedanta.
Many teachers are unaware of it too. The credit for rediscovering this
right method of Vedanta by analyzing thousands of texts goes to
Swami Satchidanandendra Saraswati, a Vedantic monk, a Sanskrit
scholar and the founder of the Adhyatma Prakasha Karyalaya in
Holenarasipura,Karnataka, India. He has written about 200 books
and spent his entire life in bringing out the exact and original
teachings of Adi Shankara .

Sat-Chit-Ananda - Truth, Consciousness, Bliss

Sat-Chit-Ananda, which means truth, consciousness and bliss is an important concept in Vedanta. This term is used to refer to the three dimensions of the absolute reality.

In Vedanta, reality has three different levels. The reality in the level of dreams and imagination is called as prathibhasika satya. If something is true only for a given time but keeps continuously changing, it is known as vyavaharika satya. Everything that is observed by the subject, everything that is physical and mental belongs to vyavaharika satya or relative reality. Finally, one that is not changing, the one that witnesses everything is the paramarthika satya or the absolute reality.

As we already discussed, as far as your conscious experience is concerned, you are the basis of the existence. You know everything that exists because you exist. So, your existence is an absolute prerequisite to know the existence of anything else. Whatever that you know as existing keeps changing; one thing that remains constant is the the subject, the observer self, the one which witnesses everything that exists. This unchanging observer is more real when you compare it with the reality of the objects which are observed. As we already discussed, in Vedanta, the definition of that which is real is the one which never changes. This unchanging absolute reality aspect is named as sat or truth.

The next word 'chit' means consciousness. The subject, the absolute reality is also conscious.It is the one which knows or the one which is aware.

The third word ananda or bliss is what liberation feels like. We all always experience the absolute reality each and every minute; in fact, every moment that you experience is the experience of Brahman. But it is clouded by our duality and ignorance. The experience of reality is not pure but it is contaminated by the clouds like delusion,hatred, greed and dissatisfaction. So, people don't taste the absolute reality in its purity as long as they are in duality. But once a person is liberated, his experience of reality is pure. This way of experiencing cannot be put into words. The word bliss is just an indication to let you know that it feels good. But it is not exactly like the experiential happiness or pleasure. It is more like an extremely peaceful, satisfied, quite ordinary, guilt-free, conflictless, self-less experience of life with a sense of innocence. It is doesn't feel like anything new but feels like something quite natural and ordinary. You also feel like you have already known it. You have a sense of wonder like a child and a mind similar to a child. It is not a distinct experience, the type which comes and goes. It is not an altered state of consciousness either. It feels more authentic and real than the conceptualized self and it feels like there is a synchronicity with the whole existence. You feel boundless and weightless. This experience of reality is ananda.

Buddha was not interested in describing absolute reality at all. He discouraged thinking about how nirvana feels like. Because, no matter how hard you try and how much intelligent you are, you cannot imagine how the nondual reality feels like, when you yourself are living in duality. This is true! But Sat-Chit-Ananda gives you an idea to work with. It gives you something that your mind can grasp.

The Three Steps of Learning - Sravana, Manana and Nididhyasana

Brihadaranyaka Upanishad 2.4.5 says:

> *"The Self, my dear Maitreyi, should be realized – should be heard of, reflected on and meditated upon;by the realization of the Self, my dear, through hearing, reflection and meditation, all this is known."*

The phrase 'should be heard of, reflected on and meditated upon' talks about three steps: Hearing, reflection and meditation. Their exact Sanskrit words are sravana, manana and nididhyasana. What do they mean?

Before we go into that, let us look at some concepts from Indian Epistemology. Each school of ancient India lists various means to acquire knowledge. There are six means in total; Vedanta school accepts all six; Yoga and Samkhya accept three. Actually, those three are sufficient since the other three can also be classified under the three primary means of knowledge. Let me explain those three primary means of knowledge.

Consider this example. A mountain is visible when you look through the window of your house. Somebody tells you that there is a forest fire behind that mountain. Just by hearing this, you have known something. But is this information reliable? It is just a verbal testimony. A verbal testimony may or may not be true. Since there is still a possibility to know something through it, verbal testimony is considered as one of the means of knowledge. It is called as shabda pramana in Sanskrit.

After hearing this, you look through the window. You see smoke above the mountain. Since you see the smoke, you can know by inference that there must be fire. But is this inference reliable? Sometimes it may not be. The smoke is probably coming because of some other reason. For example, there might be a cement factory behind the mountain which is emitting smoke. Inference still gives us the possibility of knowing something. The Sanskrit name for inference is anumana pramana.

Now, you decide to go out and reach the location behind the mountain to verify this for yourself. You see the forest fire, you see that the trees are getting burnt, you feel the heat that is coming from the fire and you are pretty sure that this is not a dream. Now you have a direct perception or direct experience of the information that was originally communicated via verbal testimony. This is very much reliable. Knowing something through direct perception or experience is called pratyaksha pramana.

There are many things in life which can be immediately known through direct experience. It doesn't necessarily have to precede by verbal testimony. But one fact about the path to liberation or the nature of absolute truth is that you can't know about it unless someone tells you first. There may be very rare individuals who got liberated accidentally. But for most of the people, somebody first have to tell them about the absolute reality. So, verbal testimony is the only means by which one can first know about it. Later on, after going through long term spiritual practice, one can know the truth by direct experience i.e by getting liberated. But this is always preceded by verbal instruction. That is why Vedanta says that scriptures are the only means of knowledge about Brahman. For example, I never knew about the path to liberation or absolute reality until I came across a book. So, it was through verbal testimony that I was informed about the path and the destination.

When you hear this verbal testimony about Brahman through a teacher, it is called Sravana, which literally means listening. The teacher instructs in such a way which directly points out the truth. In Dzogchen, a school of Tibetan Buddhism, it is called as 'rig pa'i ngo sprod' which means 'introduction to awareness or nature of mind'.

Sam Harris, a neuroscientist and the author of 'Waking up' describes his experience of receiving a pointing out instruction as follows:

> "The genius of Tulku Urgyen was that he could point out the nature of mind with the precision and matter-of-factness of teaching a person how to thread a needle and could get an ordinary meditator like me to recognize that consciousness is intrinsically free of self. There might be some initial struggle and uncertainty, depending on the student, but once the

truth of nonduality had been glimpsed, it became obvious that it was always available— and there was never any doubt about how to see it again. I came to Tulku Urgyen yearning for the experience of self-transcendence, and in a few minutes he showed me that I had no self to transcend."

When someone instructs the truth in such a way, many disciples are able to immediately get a glimpse of the truth. But usually it is just a glimpse, similar to one that I got in 2002. According to Vedanta, if one has got a perfection in the fourfold qualifications he instantly gets liberated after listening to a pointing-out instruction. But usually, people either get an intellectual understanding of the whole thing or a direct glimpse of reality for a moment, once they listen to such a spiritual instruction. It all depends on the level of the seeker.

Now, the disciple's job is to actually make this glimpse into a 24/7 reality. For this, constant repetition of the whole practice is necessary. This includes repeated witnessing and trying to remove the obstacles which keep rising. You don't allow yourself to forget it and you try to reproduce the glimpse again and again. Once you have the glimpse, it is usually very clear what you need to do. Your own inner light is capable of taking you to liberation if you constantly repeat the process of listening/reading, witnessing and getting glimpses of reality. You may go through many beautiful moments and epiphanies. Don't stop anywhere and continue with the witnessing practice. This repetition is known as manana.

Finally, when you get established as a witness 24/7, it is nididhyasana. With nididhyasana, you go deeper and deeper with unwavering attention of the thoughts, emotions, sensations, perceptions, mood changes, experiences, changes in the energy, body movements etc. This leads you to a complete detachment from the conceptualized self and finally the conceptualized self itself fades away. Nididhyasana is like perfect mindfulness.

Ramana Maharshi says:

> "By sravana, Knowledge dawns. That is the flame. By manana, the Knowledge is not allowed to vanish. Just as the flame is protected by a wind-screen, so the other thoughts are not allowed to overwhelm the right knowledge. By nididhyasana, the flame is kept up to burn bright by trimming the wick. Whenever other thoughts arise, the mind is turned inward to the light of true knowledge. When this becomes natural, it is samadhi. The enquiry "Who am I?" is the sravana. The ascertainment of the true import of 'I' is the manana. The practical application on each occasion is nididhyasana. Being as 'I' is samadhi.
>
> - Talks with Sri Ramana Maharshi, Volume III; Publisher: T.N. Venkataraman"

Ramana Maharshi taught self-inquiry. Witnessing and self-inquiry do the same thing. Witnessing and self-inquiry both come under the open-monitoring practices that we discussed before, which involves non-judgemental observation and/or inquiry into moment to moment experience.

Sri Sri Satchidanandendra Saraswati in his book Adhyatma yoga describes the process of Nididhyasana:

> "The essence of the totality of experience of the outer world is the five kinds of sensations only i . e sound, touch, form or colour, taste and smell. Except for and apart from these five sensations, there is no world as such. To prove the existence of this external world our sense organs are the only criteria. Bereft of these five-fold sensations got through the sense organs, there is no proof whatsoever available for the existence of the world. So the sense organs are 'the Self' of the external world.
>
> In this process the first step is sublating the outer world by means of the sense organs, meaning, one cognises that only through the vibrations or sensations of the sense organs one comes to experience the outer world and that there is no outer world as such apart from these sensations of the sense organs. Once having determined this, he is not drawn towards the outer world or he will not be attracted by the objects of the outer world. The result of this firm conviction is called as sublating the outer world by means of the sense organs."

The above is the first step. It helps you to turn your entire attention inward. You first recognize that everything is happening in your conscious field. All sensations of the five senses are witnessed in the field of consciousness. So, the outer world that we see is not really the outer world, but a representation of the outerworld in our inner world.

Then, we witness the manas, the part of the mind which contains hopes, dreams, fears, likes and dislikes. Swami Sri Sri Satchidanandendra Saraswati explains the second step as follows:

> "So here the Sadhaka gets a firm conviction that the mind alone appears as the sense organs and the outer world with the concepts of infinite time. space, causation, etc. This is called as the sublation of the sense organs by means of the mind. Here the Sadhaka remains in the form of the mind only. He is an embodiment of the mind, as it were. There is no independent existence for the world or sense organs apart from the mind."

As we observe the mind, we go deeper and witness the buddhi, the intellect and the discriminatory agent. The next step is basically to go beyond even Buddhi and witness how our discriminations and choices direct the mind.

Swami Sri Sri Satchidanandendra Saraswati continues:

> "Then he has to proceed inwards towards the intellect. Here the faculty of determining and objectifying the agitation of the mind is called as 'intellect' or 'Buddhi'. This intellect is the Self of the mind. By keen observation one should sublate

the mind by means of the intellect, adopting the previous way of reasoning. Here the aspirant remains as the intellect. For him there is no mind or the sense organs or the outer world independently as such, apart from the intellect."

The next step is to witness the ahankar, the feeling that 'I am the doer', the feeling of the 'I' as a separate existence. In Swamiji's words:

"Then this Sadhaka should discern or divine the stuff of the intellect i e. 'I'-sense or 'ego'. This ego objectifies the intellect in the manner: 'My intellect is capable of understanding such and such a thing or is incapable etc." Hence this 'I'-sense is the inner stuff of the intellect and also is the enjoyer of pleasure or pain. Meaning, though the pleasure and pain are related to the inner organ, this 'I'-sense identifies itself with those feelings of pleasure and pain etc. So it is called as 'enjoyer'."

Finally, your observation rises above the ego and witnesses the whole phenomenon. Swamiji continues:

"At last, the aspirant should objectify his 'I'-sense or ego taking a stand in the true nature of his own Self, that is, the Witness of the 'I'-sense. To objectify the 'I'-sense the only method is through discrimination, and with deep concentration when one says there is 'I'-sense, then automatically he takes his stand in his true nature of the Self, who is the Witness of the ego or 'I'-sense. There is no need of any effort to take a stand in the true nature of the Self,

because that is one's own nature of Being and always he is That. Due to his wrong identification with not-selves like the ego etc., one misconceives that '1 am so and so'. By adopting this process of discrimination with a concentrated mind according to this ' Adhyatma Yoga', as described here, one ceases his identification with the ego and all the rest."

What Swami Sri Sri Satchidanandendra Saraswati describes here is nothing but witnessing. He explains how you objectify and observe the contents of the consciousness. You first start by observing your sense perceptions, then observe your manas, then buddhi, and then ahankar. The above process is a perfection of witnessing which is only possible probably after many years of witnessing practice.

Swami Sri Sri Satchidanandendra Saraswati has done extensive research on the Vedantic literature and has concluded that this is nididhyasana. I have read his books and was pretty impressed with his research and analysis. His main motive was to bring out the true teachings of Shankara and explain how certain concepts were distorted by the teachers who came after Shankara.

Our intentions, Actions and Karma

Our reality is shaped by our own intentions. At every moment, we have the ability to make a choice. You determine what to do based on your intention. This intention, which is called 'chetana' in Buddhism, is the urge which makes us to think, say or do something. The kind of intention that Buddha is talking about here are the intentions which protect or enhance the self-concept or seek some kind of satisfaction or fulfillment. If you look at your past, your past is nothing but the result of your own intentions and the intentions of the others. One intention leads to another, that leads to another and it goes on endlessly. This creates a huge web of intentions. These intentions and unconscious impulses become the content of our manas. We have also created a conceptual future based on our intentions. There is a conceptual past that we have created in our mind too. The psychological sense of time along with the sense of a conceptual past and future is nothing but a creation of the manas.

We think we have freewill. But if you observe closely, the choices we make out of the so called free will are influenced by our own previous intentions. Whatever situation we have created out of our own intentions controls us. Our own free will binds us; so when we exercise our decisions, those decisions are based on the web of intentions we have in our mind, which were previously created by our free will in the first place.

So, one thing is established here: A huge part of our lives is shaped by our own intentions. And it is indeed true that we are bound by our own intentions. The influence that our own past intentions have on our current intentions and the experience of life is karma.

In Vedanta and other astika traditions, karma is all about one's actions. The word 'karma' literally means 'action'. But Buddha went one step further and noticed what caused our actions. He realized that it is our intentions which caused us to act.

Because of our intentions, we also develop mental tendencies which make us to repeatedly act in a certain way. These tendencies are called vasanas. How vasanas are formed can be explained by the psychological concept called operant conditioning, a learning process which shapes behaviours. We all already know this but I will go ahead and explain what it means. It is a simple concept: If you get rewarded in some way by doing an action, you tend to repeat that action or behaviour. if you get rewarded by not doing an action, you tend not to repeat that action. Similarly, if you can avoid a punishment (anything that is unpleasant) by doing an action, you will repeat that behaviour. if you get punished by doing an action, you will tend to avoid that action.

Let us say I like to go to a movie and I like the experience of watching the movie. The movie was entertaining and the experience was pleasant. Since I was rewarded with great experience, I would like to watch a movie again this weekend. If I keep doing this again and again, I develop a tendency or a habit to watch movies. I now have a movie vasana.

All these vasanas were developed because of our craving: Craving for sensuality, craving for becoming and craving for non-becoming. We already explored this in the first chapter. When we get liberated, the identification with these tendencies is completely broken. We no longer depend on any action for fulfillment. Your actions are restricted mostly in taking care of your basic needs and executing your responsibilities. After liberation, the actions and intentions don't create a bondage anymore because you never consider yourself as the doer. Once the illusion of a separate self dissolves, there is no more bondage no matter what actions you do or what intentions you have. But since there is no clinging to aggregates and taking them as self, you won't indulge in actions which are usually considered as immoral or hateful.

One theory that is associated with karma theory is the theory of reincarnation. According to this, karma not only binds your current life but it also leads to a rebirth after your death. The influence of karma continues to act on another person who will be born after your death. This cycle of birth and death continues until the whole karma account completely runs out. This vicious cycle is known as samsara. Liberation is believed to end this samsara.

Is reincarnation or rebirth true? We don't have any evidence for reincarnation in spite of many researches that have been done. I don't remember any past lives either. But there have been thousands of reports by many people who claim to remember a previous life. Many scientists have also done research on reincarnation. The notable one is psychiatrist Ian Stevenson. He conducted more than 2,500 interviews over a period of 40 years with people who claimed to remember past lives. Skeptics criticized his research saying that his results were influenced by confirmation bias and wishful thinking. Many scientists complained about various errors in his studies.

Terence Hines, professor of neurology at Pace University wrote the following:

"The major problem with Stevenson's work is that the methods he used to investigate alleged cases of reincarnation are inadequate to rule out simple, imaginative storytelling on the part of the children claiming to be reincarnations of dead individuals. In the seemingly most impressive cases Stevenson (1975, 1977) has reported, the children claiming to be reincarnated knew friends and relatives of the dead individual. The children's knowledge of facts about these individuals is, then, somewhat less than conclusive evidence for reincarnation"

- *Hines (2003). Pseudoscience and the Paranormal. Prometheus Books*

There are many possible reasons why someone would remember something and think that it comes from a previous birth. For example, there is a phenomenon called cryptomnesia which occurs when you recollect a forgotten memory but you don't recognize it as something you have forgotten; instead you think that it is new and original. Similarly, confabulation is a disturbance in memory which occurs when you fabricate memories, distort them or misinterpret them without a conscious intention to deceive. Then there is false memory syndrome (FMS) which happens when your identity is affected by memories that are factually incorrect but you strongly believe those memories. All these are real phenomena which have been verified by scientific research. These are not some rare disorders but common tendencies that everyone has. In other words, every person you see may sometimes recollect a forgotten memory and believe that it is something new.

Interestingly, most of the people who reported that they had memories of a previous birth are from eastern traditions which have strong belief in reincarnation or rebirth. On the contrary, there have been many people in the west who have been recognized as liberated people, but they neither had any memories of the past lives nor did they talk about rebirth. Even many liberated people from East like Ramana Maharshi and Ramakrishna Paramhamsa didn't remember their past lives even though they approved of reincarnation theory.

Does it mean reincarnation is not true? We don't have to completely reject it but accept it as a working hypothesis. But we also need to be aware of the thousands of games that our own mind is playing. The good thing is, whether reincarnation is true or not doesn't matter. You don't really need to know the truth of it to get liberated.

Even though we have made great advancement in the field of science and even though we know a lot more than what we knew 5000 years ago, we still only know less than 1% about our universe. The realm of unknown is probably 99% of everything that can be known. This may sound like an exaggeration but if you think about the vastness of the universe you can understand what I am talking about. And I don't think human race can survive long enough to know all the secrets of the universe and life.

How did our ancestors come up with reincarnation theory? Is it just a human imagination? Or is it a wishful thinking born because of the desire to be born again? Or is it some kind of truth that was discovered in deep meditation? Is it really possible to know some truth about the world just by meditating alone? What about all these supernatural powers which are talked about in all these scriptures? It all boils down to one question - Is there anything called extrasensory perception (ESP)?

James Randi, a Canadian American made an offer called 'One Million Dollar Paranormal Challenge' to pay out one million US dollars to anybody who can demonstrate a supernatural or paranormal ability under agreed-upon scientific testing criteria. The challenge was open from 1964 to 2015. Thousands of psychics applied to demonstrate their abilities but not even a single claim was proved. People who believe in ESP usually object by saying "These psychics are fake. People who really have ESP have no interest in earning money. Because, all these powers came only after they renounced their desire for money. Such people don't really show any interest in worldly things". But even though such people may not have interest in getting money for themselves, they can still use that money for charity or thousands of other social welfare activities. Money is always a need and spiritual organizations always rely on donations to keep doing their work. So, such objection really doesn't apply.

But this is not to say that such powers don't exist at all. There is no reason to be certain about it. I myself have witnessed an incident which looked like a perfect evidence for the existence of such powers. So, we can be open about such things but learn to live with uncertainty. There are millions of things in the universe which can't be explained. But when we come up with imaginary explanations for those things, it gives rise to all kinds of bogus theories. Instead of pretending that we know, it is good to learn to live with uncertainty when it comes to those things that we know nothing about. You can explore, try to know but not pretend that you already know. Also, any student of psychology knows that eye witnesses and anecdotal accounts are not reliable.

There is one thing that I need to mention here. Our own spiritual scriptures discourage the interest in or usage of paranormal powers. They say that these powers are nothing but distractions; possessing such powers can actually stop an individual from progressing further in the spiritual path. According to these scriptures, not everyone who possess paranormal powers are liberated; and not everyone who is liberated possess such powers.

Anyway, my point is, you can walk on the spiritual path, get liberated and end your suffering with 0% knowledge or experience in paranormal stuff. You don't have to know whether they are real or fake. You don't have to worry about them at all. But you may be curious about some questions: Why do certain liberated people claim to remember their past lives while other don't? Why do certain liberated people lose body consciousness in nirvikalpa samadhi while others don't go through such temporary states of samadhis at all? Why do some liberated people seem to have extra sensory perception while others don't seem to have any? If you ask this question to Ramana Maharshi, he would simply reply that it depends on one's prarabdha karma. Let us get back to the current topic of karma and learn about the different types of karma that Vedanta talks about.

Vedanta classifies karma into three types: Sanchita karma, prarabdha karma and agamya karma. Sanchita karma is the entire warehouse of your karma that you have collected over all of your previous lives. Out of the entire karmic warehouse, only a certain amount of karma is allocated to you for your current birth, which is prarabdha karma. You are supposed to exhaust this prarabdha karma in this life and you will die as soon as prarabdha karma is used up. The new karma that you create while you live is agamya karma. When a person gets liberated, the whole warehouse of sanchita karma is destroyed. He can't produce any new karma either, so there is no agamya karma. But he will live until he experiences the portion that is allocated to him for his current life. Prarabdha karma is destroyed only by experiencing it.

There is an analogy in Vedanta to explain this theory of karma. Imagine you are a bowman and you have a quiver full of arrows. The quiver of arrows represent Sanchita karma, the sum total of karma of all your past lives. Now, let us imagine you take an arrow and shoot it. The arrow you have shot represents prarabdha karma. Once the arrow is released from the bow, there is no way to stop the arrow. The arrow has to run as long as the force is exhausted. The same way, even though you can destroy all Sanchita karma at liberation, the prarabdha karma which has already begun to give fruit can't be destroyed that way. Prarabdha will get exhausted only by living the current life. Many liberated yogis talk about dying by their own will;

they just mention it as 'leaving the body', they don't call it as death. Because they claim that they can die or leave the body whenever they want, without damaging the body and without experiencing any pain. But such a concept doesn't exist in Vedanta. Of course, if prarabdha is the one which determines when you will die, you cannot determine the time of your death.

For me, some aspects of this karma theory makes sense even though I don't know for certain about reincarnation or rebirth. When you go through your spiritual practice, you are basically unwiring the knots of your mind which you have created by your own intentions. Or you can compare it with peeling the layers of an onion. When I was a seeker, I could resonate with the karma theory and I felt like my karmic load was becoming less and less. But at one point, it completely breaks the identification that you have with this load of past intentions. This is when the mental boundaries of 'me' and the 'world' breaks. The karma or whatever you want to call it is no longer yours. But those remnants of karma or past intentions still have the force to direct your actions. But they are no longer your actions now because you no longer consider yourself as the doer. So, the influence that your previous intentions have after your liberation can be compared to prarabdha karma. It works exactly like how prarabdha is supposed to work.

Buddhism also has a similar idea. There is a term called 'vipaka vinnana' that explains the karmic effect felt by people who are liberated. The concept of 'vipaka vinnana' sounds similar to prarabdha karma in Vedanta. Steven Collins is a professor in the

163

University of Chicago who works on the texts and civilizational history of Buddhism in premodern and modern South and Southeast Asia. In his book 'Selfless Persons: Imagery and Thought in Theravada Buddhism', he writes the following:

> *"However, there is still a constructed-consciousness which exists as a karmically-resultant-consciousness' (vipaka vinnana). In general, enlightened men are said to be still affected by the results of their past bad karma, although they create no new karma: the most famous example is of Moggallana, one of the Buddha's chief disciples, who — though enlightened — died a violent death as a result of having killed his parents in a former life. Each released saint preserves a particular character, an individual personality, thanks to the presence of the 'traces' or 'impregnations' of his particular karmic heritage. Of course, the very fact that there is a psycho-physical substrate during the remainder of a released saint's lifetime shows the continuing effect of karma. "*

- *'Selfless Persons: Imagery and Thought in Theravada Buddhism' by Steven Collins*

I would not recommend spending time in theoretical study of such deep concepts. It is not necessary, may cause confusion and even attachment to these theories. Whatever I have explained in this book should be sufficient for your spiritual journey. In fact, Vedanta talks about a mental tendency called 'shastra vasana' which is a trap.

Shastra vasana is nothing but the craving to read more and more theories about liberation and developing an attachment to scriptures.

Vedanta says that Vedanta itself is a superimposition. It is only used as a device to guide you towards liberation. The same concept has been conveyed by Buddha in Alagaddupama Sutta using a parable called 'raft parable':

> "Monks, I will teach you the Dhamma compared to a raft, for the purpose of crossing over, not for the purpose of holding onto. Listen & pay close attention. I will speak."

> "As you say, lord," the monks responded to the Blessed One.

> The Blessed One said: "Suppose a man were traveling along a path. He would see a great expanse of water, with the near shore dubious & risky, the further shore secure & free from risk, but with neither a ferryboat nor a bridge going from this shore to the other. The thought would occur to him, 'Here is this great expanse of water, with the near shore dubious & risky, the further shore secure & free from risk, but with neither a ferryboat nor a bridge going from this shore to the other. What if I were to gather grass, twigs, branches, & leaves and, having bound them together to make a raft, were to cross over to safety on the other shore in dependence on the raft, making an effort with my hands & feet?' Then the man, having gathered grass, twigs, branches, & leaves, having bound them together to make a raft, would

165

cross over to safety on the other shore in dependence on the raft, making an effort with his hands & feet. Having crossed over to the further shore, he might think, 'How useful this raft has been to me! For it was in dependence on this raft that, making an effort with my hands & feet, I have crossed over to safety on the further shore. Why don't I, having hoisted it on my head or carrying it on my back, go wherever I like?' What do you think, monks: Would the man, in doing that, be doing what should be done with the raft?"

"No, lord."

"And what should the man do in order to be doing what should be done with the raft? There is the case where the man, having crossed over, would think, 'How useful this raft has been to me! For it was in dependence on this raft that, making an effort with my hands & feet, I have crossed over to safety on the further shore. Why don't I, having dragged it on dry land or sinking it in the water, go wherever I like?' In doing this, he would be doing what should be done with the raft. In the same way, monks, I have taught the Dhamma compared to a raft, for the purpose of crossing over, not for the purpose of holding onto. Understanding the Dhamma as taught compared to a raft, you should let go even of Dhammas, to say nothing of non-Dhammas.

- "Alagaddupama Sutta: The Water-Snake Simile" (MN 22), translated from the Pali by Thanissaro Bhikkhu.

Scriptures and spiritual teachings are similar to a boat that helps you to reach the other shore. They should be only used to reach the other shore and there should not be any clinging. There are many people who spend their entire lives in discussing and debating about scriptures. This is a big trap, so watch out for it.

We can compare Buddhism and Vedanta to two languages that evolved from a parent proto-language. As centuries passed and as different concepts evolved in each school, they became like two mutually unintelligible languages which belong to the same parent. It is also possible that schools like samkhya and buddhism evolved from the same proto-school of thought. Vedanta uses a certain teaching method called Adhyaropa Apavada while Buddhism teaches directly and precisely. Vedanta is poetic where as Buddhism is empirical. Buddhism gives you the raw truth but Vedanta offers to you with added sweets and flavors. The big problem in Vedanta is that people may get stuck with the words, concepts and theories.

Here is a poem that I wrote which has many pointers. It puts Vedantic teachings in a nutshell:

You are the Truth

Carrying the weight of past in my head

And dragging the scenes which were old and dead,

The Truth About Spiritual Enlightenment

I ran to grab the bliss of the future;

The more I ran, the more was the torture..

The torture of the hedonic treadmill

Followed me as I continued uphill;

I was caught in the prison of craving

With tedious thoughts, my mind was raving.

I met an ugly old man on the way

who had a long thick beard with shades of grey.

His face was shining with heavenly bliss;

In his eyes I saw an endless abyss!

"What makes you so happy in this rat race?",

I asked him as he slowly turned his face.

He replied,"The answer is within you!

The grand kingdom of God is within you!"

"That's a joke", I said "Are you kidding me?".

"No!" He said, "Turn inward, you'll become free!

You've made your own boundaries inside your mind,

You've closed your eyes and think you've become blind".

I said, "How can I get out of this trap?

I want to find the way, give me the map"

He said, "You're the way, the truth and the life!

Be still and know you're that, and end this strife!

You're not your body and you're not your mind;

Not knowing the timeless truth makes you blind;

You're not your story and you're not your thoughts;

You're not those age old, buried mental knots.

You're not that chattering voice in your head;

You're not anything that you did or said;

You're not anything that you have or know

You're the truth that is watching all this show!

The Truth About Spiritual Enlightenment

You're not anything that can be perceived;

You're not an object that can be observed;

You're the screen where the world is being played;

You're the emptiness where the form is made.

You're the one witnessing the mind and breath;

You're one without two, beyond birth and death;

Like the air trapped in a small round bubble,

You feel separate which brings all the trouble.

Inquire inside and wake up from this dream!

Let truth alone shine like a bright white beam!

By inquiry, your illusions will break;

You'll stop mistaking the rope for a snake"

Hearing these words stopped my thoughts for a while.

Looking in, I slowly began to smile.

I watched my thoughts as they slowly passed by;

I observed my mind like a secret spy.

For years, I contemplated on his words;

I watched my thoughts fly like a bunch of birds.

One day, I woke up and realized the truth;

Since then my life has been peaceful and smooth!

Chapter Ten: Bridging Science and Spirituality

In this chapter, I am going to list various studies and books written by scientists who have done some serious research on liberation, spiritual experiences and the causes of human suffering. You can skip this chapter if you are not really a fan of science or read it later if you want to. You can also read the conclusion given at the end which gives you a quick summary of everything that is explained in this chapter.

One of my intentions for writing this book is to emphasize that science and spirituality should be bridged. We have been seeing a lot of con artists who exploit and abuse people in the name of spirituality. Spirituality has also become a good way for cult leaders to conduct their business. For the last 3000 years, so many things have been written about spiritual enlightenment or liberation which have added a lot of confusions and myths to spirituality. It is very hard for common people to separate facts from the myths. In this century, there has been a huge awareness about spirituality all over the world and enlightenment has become a popular niche for authors and speakers. Certainly, a serious empirical research about human liberation is necessary and such studies have been already carried out by many people around the world. This chapter will give you an outline of the important observations that have been made by these scientists.

Human Brain

Before we talk about spirituality in scientific terms, it is necessary to understand a little bit about human brain. Your brain has specialized cells called 'neurons' which communicate with other neurons through electrochemical signals called 'Action potentials'. Everything we think, feel and experience is the result of the constant activity in the neural network of your brain.

Let us talk about two distinct parts of the brain - the higher and lower. The upper part of the brain, that is involved in higher cognitive functions is divided into four lobes - Frontal (just behind your forehead), parietal (second half of the top part of your brain, behind the frontal lobe), occipital lobe (in the back of your head) and temporal lobe (two sides of the head, near the ears). Frontal lobe is responsible for executive functions like planning, analysing etc. It has a structure called neocortex which is the recently evolved part of the brain. Your brain also has a lower part that includes limbic system, brainstem and hindbrain which take care of the basic functions of the brain like arousal, sleep, hunger etc. It also prepares the brain to face a threat and initiates the flight or fight response. Amygdala in this region is responsible for emotions such as fear; hippocampus is responsible for forming new memories. This whole lower part is the oldest part of the brain which reminds us that we are essentially animals.

Your upper brain, the cerebral lobes, can be divided into two hemispheres. Each hemisphere dominate the other in certain cognitive functions. This phenomenon is called lateralization of the brain. A very important distinction is language. Your left hemisphere plays a major role in language production and understanding the language.

The Left brain interpreter - The creator of duality and the cause of suffering

Now, let us try to understand what creates the separation between 'you' and the rest of the world. This basic categorization is done by our left brain and it can be explained by something called left-brain interpreter. This is what creates categories like 'you' vs world, self image vs ideal self, good vs bad etc. The categorization of 'you' vs 'world' becomes very solid in the long run, as a result of learning and neuroplasticity.

To give you a brief introduction of this left brain interpreter, let me quote from Wikipedia:

"The left brain interpreter refers to the construction of explanations by the left brain in order to make sense of the world by reconciling new information with what was known before. The left brain interpreter attempts to rationalize, reason and generalize new information it receives in order to relate the past to the present. The concept was first introduced by Michael Gazzaniga while he performed research on split-brain patients during the early 1970s with Roger Sperry at the California Institute of Technology. Sperry eventually received the 1981 Nobel Prize in Medicine for his contributions to split-brain research

The drive to seek explanations and provide interpretations is a general human trait, and the left brain interpreter can be seen as the glue that attempts to hold the story together, in order to provide a sense of coherence to the mind. In reconciling the past and the present, the left brain interpreter may confer a sense of comfort to a person, by providing a feeling of consistency and continuity in the world. This may in turn produce feelings of security that the person knows how "things will turn out" in the future.

However, the facile explanations provided by the left brain interpreter may also enhance the opinion of a person about themselves and produce strong biases which prevent the person from seeing themselves in the light of reality and repeating patterns of behavior which led to past failures. The *explanations generated by the left brain interpreter may be balanced by right brain systems which follow the constraints of reality to a closer degree. The suppression of the right hemisphere by electroconvulsive therapy leaves patients inclined to accept conclusions that are absurd but based on strictly-true logic. After electroconvulsive therapy to the left hemisphere the same absurd conclusions are indignantly rejected."*

Chris Niebauer is a neuroscientist who received his Ph.D. in Cognitive Neuropsychology from the University of Toledo where he specialized in left-right brain differences. He has written a book called 'The Neurotic's Guide to Avoiding Enlightenment: How the Left-brain Plays Unending Games of Self-improvement' in which he explains this left-brain interpreter in detail. This book is based on the teachings of Eckhart Tolle and attempts to integrate his teachings with neuroscience. Let me quote a few lines from his book:

"The interpreter in the left brain has a preference for consistency and little tolerance for ambiguity. There are right and wrong answers and things need to be predictable and orderly. Paradox is a turn-off to interpreter. Left brain is so based in categories, it categorizes everything as right and wrong, good and bad. Categories divide and the interpreter has divided itself into 'How i am' and 'how i want to be' "

"The left-brain interpreter is categorical, it creates division outwardly and inwardly, so let it do its job, let it do its thing. Here we might ask why you want to go beyond your ego and more importantly, is it your ego that wants this? Because if it is, it can't. Going beyond the ego is nothing like what the ego thinks it is, how could it be? When the ego tries to drag itself beyond itself it may bring along a little anxiety and conflict, so remember that all scary things are pretend. Also, Alan pointed out in the 70s that the biggest ego trip of all was in believing that one was beyond the ego. Today this is also true but with one more level to it, today there is the ego trip of pointing out that the 6i:4:est ego trip of all is in believing you have gone beyond the ego. The notion that you can improve yourself by going beyond your ego stems directly from the interpretive mind, and as such, is an interpretation that something is wrong and there is something that needs be done about it. Again, there is the interpreter created category of "me as I am" vs. "me as I want to be" which are both just thoughts bouncing around in the skull. So, ironically, if you are trying to improve yourself, you can't. The notion that your self needs improving is an interpretation and we are going around interpretations. There is an irony in most bookstores called the "self help" section. I might suggest renaming this as "Books that reinforce the illusion that the left-brain interpreter can be what it isn't free of itself."

> *"The interpreter also creates and sustains our collection of categorical thoughts called our beliefs."*

- *From 'The Neurotic's Guide to Avoiding Enlightenment: How the Left-brain Plays Unending Games of Self-improvement' by Chris Niebauer*

Here the story of Dr. Jill Bolte Taylor is worth mentioning. She is a Harvard-trained and published neuroanatomist who experienced a severe hemorrhage in the left hemisphere of her brain in 1996. This permanently changed her perception of reality.

She says, "It was as though my mind had shifted away from my normal perception of reality—where I'm the person on the machine having the experience—to some esoteric space where I'm witnessing myself having this experience."

"My perception of physical boundaries was no longer limited to where my skin met air," she has written in her memoir, "My Stroke of Insight". The core message of the book is that people can choose to live a more peaceful, spiritual life by sidestepping their left brain.

As we see, the interpreter plays a major role in dividing the reality. It also creates a split between our self-image and our ideal self. We all have a self-concept which consists of various beliefs about who we are and what we want to be. As clear borders have been defined for this egoic identity, there is a constant need to protect and enhance this identity. Most of our suffering results from our constant identification with this conceptual entity by giving it a solid reality in our minds. A threat to the self-concept or self-image is perceived by our body and mind like any other threat in the world (like a threat faced by an animal of being killed). So, all of such experiences create the same physiological reactions by activating the amygdala and initiating a fight-or-flight response. We are also in a constant pursuit of enhancing the self-concept by accumulating wealth, knowledge and beliefs about ourselves. We depend on our past to define who we are and we depend on the future to enhance it. Because of this, we are stuck in a hedonic treadmill.

Neural Correlates of the egoic self

To study about the enlightenment in neuroscientific perspective we have to know about a neural network called 'The Default Mode Network' in the brain.

The default mode network (DMN) refers to the structures in the brain which are active when we are not focused on any task in particular. If you are idle, this network is activated by default. This network is activated when we are mind wandering, thinking about others, thinking about one's self, remembering the past, and envisioning the future. This network has everything to do with the egoic self that we are identified with. The main structures of default mode network are precuneus, posterior cingulate cortex, medial prefrontal cortex and certain other areas.

The solid entity of 'me and my story' categorized by the left-brain interpreter has a need to be enhanced and protected. The whole process of enhancing and protecting this entity can be observed as a constant activity in the default mode network during the resting state of the brain. This activity can in turn feed and activate the left-brain interpreter again.

Excessive activity in default mode network has been correlated with depression. It has also been found that decreased activity in default mode network correlates with increased happiness.
Based my own experience and according to various studies done on mindfulness meditation, I can say mindfulness reduces the activity in default mode network and changes the perception of self. The practice of Buddhist mindfulness, witnessing and inquiring on the nature of your mind ultimately leads to removing the psychological boundaries of 'me' and the 'world'.

Neural mechanisms of suffering

Dr. Rick Hanson, Ph.D, a clinical psychologist, has written a wonderful book called 'Buddha's Brain: The Practical Neuroscience of Happiness, Love & Wisdom'. In this book, he has attempted to bridge science with the traditional Buddhist teachings. He explains the neural mechanisms of suffering and explains how, by meditation, one can bring neuroplastic changes in the brain and end suffering.

So, what exactly happens when our brain perceives a threat to our self-image?. Our brain regards it as a danger and activates the amygdala. Here is how he describes it:

> "Something happens. It might be a car suddenly cutting you off, a put-down from a coworker, or even just a worrisome thought. Social and emotional conditions can pack a wallop like physical ones since psychological pain draws on many of the same neural networks as physical pain (Eisenberger and Lieberman 2004); this is why getting rejected can feel as bad as a root canal. Even just anticipating a challenging event— such as giving a talk next week—can have as much impact as living through it for real. Whatever the source of the threat, the amygdala sounds the alarm, setting off several reactions: The thalamus—the relay station in the middle of your head—sends a "Wake up!" signal to your brain stem, which in turn releases stimulating norepinephrine throughout your brain. norepinephrine throughout your brain. The SNS sends signals to the major organs and muscle groups in your body, readying them for fighting or fleeing. The hypothalamus—the brain's primary regulator of the endocrine system—prompts the pituitary gland to signal the adrenal glands to release the "stress hormones"epinephrine (adrenaline) and cortisol.

Within a second or two of the initial alarm, your brain is on red alert, your SNS is lit up like a Christmas tree, and stress hormones are washing through your blood. In other words, you're at least a little upset. What's going on in your body? Epinephrine increases your heart rate (so your heart can move more blood) and dilates your pupils (so your eyes gather more light). Norepinephrine shunts blood to large muscle groups. Meanwhile, the bronchioles of your lungs dilate for increased gas exchange—enabling you to hit harder or run faster. Cortisol suppresses the immune system to reduce inflammation from wounds. It also revs up stress reactions in two circular ways: First, it causes the brain stem to stimulate the amygdala further, which increases amygdala activation of the SNS/HPAA system—which produces more cortisol. Second, cortisol suppresses hippocampal activity (which normally inhibits the amygdala); this takes the brakes off the amygdala, leading to yet more cortisol. Reproduction is sidelined—no time for sex when you're running for cover. The same for digestion: salivation decreases and peristalsis slows down, so your mouth feels dry and you become constipated. Your emotions intensify, organizing and mobilizing the whole brain for action. SNS/HPAA arousal stimulates the amygdala, which is hardwired to focus on negative information and react intensely to it. Consequently, feeling stressed sets you up for fear and anger. As limbic and endocrine activation increases, the relative strength of executive control from the PFC declines. It's like being in a car with a runaway accelerator: the driver has less control over her vehicle. Further, the PFC is also affected by SNS/HPAA arousal, which pushes appraisals, attributions of others' intentions, and priorities in a negative direction: now the driver of the careening car thinks everybody else is an idiot. For example, consider the difference between your take on a situation when you're upset and your thoughts about it later when you're calmer. In the harsh physical and social environments in which we evolved, this activation of multiple bodily systems helped our ancestors survive. But what's the cost of this today, with the chronic low-grade stresses of modern life? "

- *Buddha's Brain: The Practical Neuroscience of Happiness, Love & Wisdom' by Dr. Rick Hanson, Ph.D*

This constant 'SNS/HPAA arousal' (Sympathetic nervous system – hypothalamic-pituitary-adrenocortical axis) when a threat is perceived for this 'egoic self' is the reason why we go through unnecessary stress and suffering. Practices like mindfulness shrinks amygdala and inhibits SNS/HPAA arousal. Many years of mindfulness practice combined with insights of reality produces neuroplastic changes in the brain which results in spiritual enlightenment.

In addition to this Rick also explains how a duality is created:

- *"The parietal lobes of the brain are located in the upper back of the head (a "lobe" is a rounded swelling of the cortex). For most people, the left lobe establishes that the body is distinct from the world, and the right lobe indicates where the body is compared to features in its environment. The result is an automatic, underlying assumption along the lines of I am separate and independent. Although this is true in some ways, in many important ways it is not.*

- *Since we are each connected and interdependent with the world, our attempts to be separate and independent are regularly frustrated, which produces painful signals of disturbance and threat."*

  - *Buddha's Brain: The Practical Neuroscience of Happiness, Love & Wisdom' by Dr. Rick Hanson, Ph.D*

Persistent Non-Symbolic Experiences

Dr. Jeffery A. Martin is a founder of the Transformative Technology space, serial entrepreneur and social scientist who researches personal transformation and the states of greatest human well-being. He spent the last 10 years conducting the largest international study on persistent non-symbolic experience (PNSE), which includes the types of consciousness commonly known as: enlightenment, nonduality, the peace that passeth understanding, unitive experience, and hundreds of others. More recently, he has used this research to make systems available to help people obtain profound psychological benefits in a rapid, secular, reliable, and safe way.

He has done research on over 1200 participants (who claim to be enlightened) all over the world and he has made many publications. He has documented various traits that he has observed in enlightened people in his paper 'Clusters of Individual Experiences form a Continuum of Persistent Non-Symbolic Experiences in Adults'. You can find his paper at http://nonsymbolic.org/publications/

Other scientists who were involved

Apart from the ones that I have mentioned, there are many other scientists who have done research on this topic and have written books about it.

Arthur J. Deikman, who was a clinical professor of psychiatry at the University of California did a lot of research on the subject and coined a term called 'Mystical psychosis'. This term is used to to characterize first-person accounts of psychotic experiences that are strikingly similar to reports of mystical experiences. When Arthur himself went through a mystical experience, he became more interested in this subject. You can find many of his articles on his website http://www.deikman.com. An article named 'Awareness' explains the non-dual awareness in detail.

Modern scientists like Culadasa and Sam Harris are also worth mentioning. They have written books about meditations and spiritual awakenings. The book 'Waking up -A Guide to Spirituality Without Religion ' written by Sam Harris is an excellent scientific introduction to human liberation. He is an atheist and a skeptic but he has studied under various spiritual teachers and went through many epiphanies,

Abraham Maslow's theory of self-actualization is the earliest description in psychology about the ultimate human potential, which is very close to self-realization. William James, an early psychologist has studied various spiritual experiences and has written a book about it.

Conclusion

After going through various books and studies, I came up with a rough explanation for spiritual awakening in scientific terminology. The following is the short summary of everything that we learnt in this chapter:

> *Enlightenment is all about removing the duality, the solid psychological distinction between 'me' and the 'other' or 'me' vs 'world'. People who are spiritually enlightened feel that their experience of the reality is nondual and they don't derive a separate sense of an egoic self based on their life story and their self-concept.*

So, it all boils down to one thing – Change in the perception of self.

Now, let us try to understand what creates the separation between 'you' and the rest of the world. This basic categorization is done by our left brain and it can be explained by something called left-brain interpreter. This is what creates categories like 'you' vs world, self image vs ideal self, good vs bad etc. The categorization of 'you' vs 'world' becomes very solid in the long run, as a result of learning and neuroplasticity.

The interpreter plays a major role in dividing the reality. It also creates a split between our self-image and our ideal self. We all have a self-concept which consists of various beliefs about who we are and what we want to be. As clear borders have been defined for this egoic identity, there is a constant need to protect and enhance this identity.

Most of our suffering results from our constant identification with this conceptual entity by giving it a solid reality in our minds. A threat to the self-concept or self-image is perceived by our body and mind like any other threat in the world (like a threat faced by an animal of being killed). So, all of such experiences create the same physiological reactions by activating the amygdala and initiating a fight-or-flight response.

We are also in a constant pursuit of enhancing the self-concept by accumulating wealth, knowledge and beliefs about ourselves. We depend on our past to define who we are and we depend on the future to enhance it. Because of this, we are stuck in a hedonic treadmill.

Spiritual enlightenment promises to end suffering by ending this hedonic treadmill. It leads one to resolve all the internal conflicts and to feel one with everything. It removes the idea that there is a separate entity inside which has to enhance itself for fulfillment. The left brain may still continue to categorize things, but they are not solidified in our consciousness and urge us to protect those solidified entities.

Chapter Eleven: The Journey Of A Seeker - My Story

This chapter is about my own spiritual journey. This is not a complete autobiographical sketch of my life. I have not talked much about my personal life and have left out a whole bunch of details which have got nothing to do with spirituality. But I have tried to include everything that happened in my life which are related to my spiritual progress.

Early years

I grew up in a Hindu family which required me to believe in a personal God and his family of Gods. My grandparents taught me that God had a family with children who had God relatives. I was asked to pray to them to have my wishes granted and threatened to be punished by God if I was morally wrong. My early childhood days were spent in listening to stories of mythology and singing devotional songs. I showed more devotion than any of the other children of my age in my neighborhood. Eventually, I began to fall in love with all these heavenly beings and had a deep desire to see them with my physical eyes. I was told that it was possible if I prayed enough.

In those early days, I have watched movies in which devotees performed Tapas (penance) to get a vision of God and to get their boons granted. They were shown to be sitting or standing with closed eyes in various positions for years with no food and water so that they can have such visions. Seeing those people in movies, I too tried to imitate them. I used to sit with closed eyes for fifteen to thirty minutes every day when I was seven years old. Unknowingly, I had tried to do my first meditation this way.

I had learnt to read very early in my life. When I was seven years old, I could read and understand stories in children's magazines written in Tamil. This was going to help to me to learn some advanced topics in the years to come. The same year, I was also taught in school about Buddha. I was taught that Buddha attained enlightenment under a bodhi tree and I had no idea what it meant.

Introduction to the Books of Ramakrishna Paramahamsa

When I was about nine years old, I happened to read the book 'Gospel Of Ramakrishna'. Ramakrishna Paramahamsa was the guru of Swami Vivekananda. He was considered to be enlightened but was not as famous as Vivekananda. I was fascinated about the trances that Ramakrishna used to go through, a state in which he was immersed in divine bliss with no consciousness of the outside world. The trances are called Samadhis. I also read about the unbelievable stories of how he used to have visions of Goddess Kali and talk with her. His words were filled with pearls of wisdom. One thing he insisted was to stay away from women and gold. He considered the desires for women and gold to be the common obstacles to spiritual enlightenment. (Obviously, his advice was according to how he lived his life and this has been generalized for everyone. I would not suggest anyone to stay away from women. Such forced self - control, especially if it is against your own nature or personality, is dangerous. Any non-attachment should happen naturally by bringing in more awareness to your mind).

Reading this book increased my desire to see God in a physical form. Ramakrishna used to say that if somebody sheds tears in the desire to see God, then he would definitely see God in this lifetime and attain liberation (enlightenment). Reading this, I immediately shed tears after shutting myself in the pooja (worship) room.

I was also impressed about the fact that Ramakrishna followed Christianity and Islam to see if they also led to the same goal of Samadhi. He was able to get the same results by doing sadhana in Christian and Sufi paths.

Exposure to Yoga and Other Concepts

After a year, I started reading a book about Yoga and came to know about Ashtanga yoga, the eight limbs of Yoga in the path of attaining Samadhi. Samadhi is the highest goal of Yoga but it requires years and years of practising meditation, doing asanas and pranayamas (exercises manipulating the breath). I tried to do meditation often but ended up fighting with my thoughts and had no success in concentration. After seeing continuous failures in getting my mind to focus on a single object, I finally gave up the confidence that I could do it.

Then I started reading Bhagwad Gita and Periya Puranam (A collection of stories of 63 enlightened devotees of Lord Shiva). I had also read a few mythological books including Skanda Purana and Shiva Purana. I also read texts about Vedanta and self-inquiry but I could not understand them. Finally, I started to believe that God is one, formless but can show himself to devotees in the form they worship.

When I read more about science, I understood that many of the things which are in the spiritual domain are not accepted by science. One day I thought, 'May be I should do something to create a bridge between science and religion'. I always dreamed of becoming a scientist when I was a child. I believed that if religion is approached in a scientific way, we can discover many things.

Teenage Years

During my teenage years, I developed depression and inferiority complex. I had trouble in forming friendships and I saw myself as unworthy. But I had a lot of ambitions. I had mastered the art of writing poetry in Tamil in classical metres like venba, asiriyappa, virtutham etc. I was known as a good poet and orator in my school, by the time I was 14 years old. Even though I had inferiority complex, I had absolutely no stage fear.

But my depression deepened in the coming months and I began to show some abnormal behaviour in school. I used to shut myself in a classroom and cry without any reason. I also developed a crush on a girl and started convincing myself that it was love. I lived far away from reality and had developed a fantasy prone and neurotic personality. I clearly showed the traits of bipolar disorder. I used to be known as the most brilliant student in my class. But the depressive phases and my so called 'love' had made me to seek more time in solitude. After recovering from depression to some extent and finishing my tenth grade, I wrote hundreds of poems about love, life and God during the summer vacation. By this time, I had also formed an image of an ideal self, a self that I wanted to be. Everybody has an actual self and an ideal self. The less they overlap with each other, the more anxiety they feel. My actual self and ideal self didn't seem to even touch each other.

First, I wanted to be seen as normal by people and conform to the standards of society. I wanted to develop my social skills and interact with people with confidence. Then I wanted to be known as an accomplished poet or an author in the future. Finally, I wanted to marry the girl I loved and live happily ever after. Before I die, I wanted to make sure that my name is registered in the history. That was my ideal self. I realized I had to work really hard to achieve my goals.

Also, when I looked back on what I read about Yoga and attaining Samadhi, I realized that was not going to be possible. How can I ever stop my desire for money, women and other things? After all, everyone is striving for well being. If I stop going for things that will increase my well being, then what else I would do to bring myself lasting happiness? I realized that spirituality was not for me.

College Years

I lived away from my parents when I was studying in a polytechnic college in Chennai. I initially stayed in a hostel but due to pathological ragging that was done by seniors in the hostel, I moved to a room shared with other students. I faced a lot of issues during those times but I have just made the long story short. I had chosen to study chemical technology but unfortunately in a few months I realized that it was not the subject I wanted to study. So, for the first year and a half, I did not score well in the exams.

In the fourth semester I took a decision. I decided to dedicate myself to studies, accomplish my goals and show ultimate devotion to God to earn his grace. I also tried to be morally perfect in every aspect. If God chooses to show his grace to people who are moral and devotional, then it should happen to me. So, I pushed myself to the extreme. The life for the 6 months was very intense and I gave my 100% in everything, in every moment of life.

During mid December of that year, I started to walk 2 kilometres in the morning at 4 am everyday to a nearby temple and pray for about an hour. Then I would walk back to my room. I did the same thing in the evening and I continued this for a month.

Here is the gist of my prayers: "Dear God.. you know me very well and you are aware of what I can do and what I cannot do. I am trying all I could do to change myself, work hard and also be a good person. But I have difficulty in controlling my impulses and exercising self-control. Why did you create me like this, with this kind of genetics? Please show me the way.. I don't know what else to do. I have what you have given me as my available resources.. You gave me this body, you gave me these tendencies.. How can I alone be responsible to correct those tendencies and be a good, kind, hardworking person? You gave me the environment and genetic factors that made me neurotic, selfish and irresponsible. I tried my best and I am not able to change that. Is it fair if you punish me for something that I don't have full control over? Please be kind and help me"..

I literally used to have a mental conversation with God everyday in the temple. In the meantime, I started analyzing my thoughts and behaviors seriously. Every time I behaved in a negative way, I sat and analyzed what went wrong. I made my thought process conscious and engaged in a deep contemplation every day.

In the meantime I started to wonder how much control an individual has over one's behavior. Consider the following facts:

- People with low levels of serotonin, a neurotransmitter produced by the nervous system, are predisposed to show impulsive activity and emotional aggression.
- People who have high levels of testosterone are more likely to show aggressive behavior.
- A brain tumor caused an individual to be sexually abusive towards girls. Once the tumor was removed, he became normal. Here is the entire story: There was a male teacher in Virginia. In 2000, he began to read sex magazines, watch child porn and tried to molest his young step daughter. He was arrested and sentenced to the prison. He tried to commit suicide the day before being sentenced to jail. When doctors diagnosed the reasons for the problem, they found out that there was an egg-sized brain tumor. Once it was removed, he began alright and such impulses disappeared. This has been published in the Journal of the American Medical Association (JAMA) titled 'Right orbitofrontal tumor with pedophilia symptom and constructional apraxia sign' (Burns & Swerdlow, 2003).

These psychological findings show that a person's behaviour is highly influenced by hereditary factors, hormonal levels, other biological factors and the environment. They can even affect self control. So, somebody's moral behaviour is not completely under his or her control. Those days I used to think, "So, If God created me like this, is it fair for God to punish me for the behaviour that is simply the result of my biology? Also, what kind of God he is if he chooses to favour the people who pray to him? I am willing to change and trying my best, so what is stopping from God to help me?". My mind was filled with all these questions.

I used to put these questions to God when I prayed. I reasoned with him a lot and I told him I really had no idea what to do more than what I was doing then. Whatever the problem was, I asked God to fix it. If it seemed impossible for any reason, I asked him to take my life and give me eternal peace.

When it came to studies, I made sure I dedicated a few hours each day. I pushed myself too hard and started to bite off more than I could chew, in all aspects. I remained alert about my thought patterns and behaviors and constantly monitored myself. I could manage all this until the end of the semester. After that, there was no way I could continue doing what I was doing. The grip that I had over myself began to loosen and I started losing my self control.

I did really well in the exams that semester. I had got the third highest score among my peers. But I had expected to come first. I did all I could do for this. I obviously worked harder than others but I still couldn't reach my goal. My ideal self appeared to be so far away. I felt restless, anxious and unhappy.

In the next 6 months, I experienced a tremendous fear of loss. I started to get thoughts like, 'what if I lost everything I have, What if I become a beggar?'.... I didn't resist those thoughts, instead I waited to see what those thoughts are up to. Whatever bad situation that I imagined, I made myself mentally strong to face it. I told myself 'I can face anything in my life!'... One of my favorite proverbs those days was 'Hope for the best but prepare for the worst'..

I gradually started questioning everything in my life.. What is the purpose of this life after all? Why should I continue to live? Everything seemed to be meaningless. My rational mind started to question the existence of God. When I dug deeper into my mind, it seemed as if nothing had any purpose. There seemed to be no way to fulfill the expectations of mind. I thought I would rather die instead of having to suffer with my immature, neurotic and unpredictable personality.

Then I thought, 'If I have decided to end this life now, then I have a freedom of doing anything I like... I can die at any minute when it seems to be impossible to live any longer.'... The idea that death is an open choice all the time gave me a sudden sense of freedom and peace. 'Let me let this life going and see what happens' I thought.

Introduction to the books of Osho

I got a membership in a nearby library later that year, in my fifth semester. That is where I saw a book by Osho. I had heard about him before but had no idea who he was and what he taught. So, I borrowed that book and began to read.

The first thing that caught my attention was what he said about meditation. He said that trying to concentrate and fighting with thoughts generate more and more thoughts as a result. He made very clear that meditation was not concentration. (he was not a fan of focused meditations). He suggested a new technique for meditation which was to witness my thoughts non-judgmentally, as an observer. He taught to observe my thoughts as if I had nothing to do with them. I was kind of already doing this and I felt it very easy and doable.

Next, he said that God is not a person. There is no personal God. 'That is what I thought', I said to myself. He told that there is Godliness, which is the very essence of life, which is the very essence of who I am.

Third, He made very clear what ego is. One of the things that both shocked me and sounded true was the fact that even trying to be humble can be a subtle way for ego to show superiority over others. We tend to think we are more humble than others and that kind of gives us a humble ego. You may think that you are the greatest devotee of God and it gives you a devotional ego. All these are ego's attempt to show you in a positive light. He made me aware that ego tries to find meaning in everything and attaches itself to it. It makes me to define myself with concepts and always makes me in a constant pursuit of enhancing itself. It maintains a story, the story of 'me' and makes us constantly to be identified with it and protect it all the time. He also revealed that cutting off of the identification with this self-concept created by ego is enlightenment. It is just realizing our own nature which is hidden behind the veil of ego. That is what Buddha realized under Bodhi tree. That is what Ramakrishna found in Samadhi. That is what every individual is searching for. That true nature of yours is what people actually call God. God is not somebody who is sitting in the heaven, watching you and granting your wishes and answering your prayers. Everybody has a potential to realize their true nature.

I realized that a new door was opened for me. A new possibility of attaining complete fulfilment in my life had been just revealed to me. I found it to be refreshing, exciting and illuminating. I continued to read many books of Osho and became addicted to it. In one of his books, he revealed his own story of enlightenment and how it happened to him.

Here is a list of facts and teachings revealed by Osho, a gist of what I understood from many books I read after that:

- As you start witnessing your thoughts and be alert each and every moment, you will start noticing gaps between thoughts. The gaps will get bigger and you will soon be able to witness your unconscious patterns, emotions, moods and subtle sensations. Gradually your thoughts will reduce and you will come to a point where there is absolute stillness. Then suddenly, when you are least expecting anything to happen, enlightenment happens.

- Then you realize you are what you have been searching for. Your true nature which is beyond space and time is revealed to you which leaves you absolutely blissful and content.

- If you try to become a morally good person by extreme self-control, it leads to suppressing your desires. Then you will become a hypocrite. You will be a good person at the periphery, but in the center all those tendencies that cause immoral behavior will exist and erupt at anytime. But once you are enlightened, you will naturally be a good person.

- The presence of an enlightened person radiates peace and love, and has the ability to quieten your mind. If you get to live near an enlightened person, your spiritual progress will naturally accelerate.

- Love is another path to enlightenment. You can either start with witnessing or love.

- If you pay attention to what you are doing and witness everything that happens inside you, than anything that you do is a meditation. Simple things like walking, eating will become a meditation if you are mindful, alert and witness every thought, sensation and activity that happens. It is important to have a non judgemental attitude.

- When you live moment to moment like this, you will simply do what is required at the given moment. Preoccupation with past and future disappears. There will not be even necessary to make plans for the future. You will be absolutely satisfied with whatever the present moment brings to you.

- He gave a controversial discourse series called 'From Sex to superconsciousness' in which he said being mindful during sex can be a good meditation and become a doorway for enlightenment.

- He insisted that there is no need to renounce the world to be spiritually enlightened. One can become enlightened by living a normal life as a householder.

- Phrases like 'achieving enlightenment' or 'becoming enlightened' are actually wrong because we are already what we are looking for. We just have to realize or uncover that. He made very clear that words can be misleading and they are just like a finger pointing to the moon.

I noticed a style in Osho. Osho had a tendency to exaggerate things. When he narrated an event that happened in the life of somebody who was enlightened, he often made his own screenplay and dialogues and made the story very dramatic.

Also, he said many times that what he talks in his discourses is not at all important. His discourse is simply a device to silence our minds and make us receptive to his presence. Once we are receptive and available to his presence, then it can directly work on the seekers to progress in the path. He insisted more on a silent transmission than the content of his talks.

He also insisted that enlightenment should not be seen as a goal. That is a subtle way of ego entering through the backdoor. Enlightenment is not an achievement; it is simply uncovering our true nature. Everybody has the potential for it. But a desire for enlightenment can also be the final hindrance to enlightenment. At one point, you may need to drop even the desire for enlightenment, which happens at the last step. The whole spiritual path is a tricky way of making your self-concept dissolve and stopping you from craving. The desire for enlightenment is also a desire! But it will automatically drop at the last step.

He has contradicted himself many times and has openly admitted it. He would say that life is full of contradictions and he is vast enough to contain all the contradictions. Sometimes it is natural for his statements to seem like contradictions. But whenever somebody asked about a contradiction, he often explained it to prove that in fact there was no contradiction.

But there were also some real obvious contradictions in the talks of Osho. When a disciple asked about such things while he was in the US, he said, 'In the beginning I couldn't tell you the truth directly. Because, you were clinging to the past and didn't want to hear the truth. So I just used your old leaders of the past to convey what I wanted to say. Now I can directly talk to you and say what I want to say without any cheating. So, always consider my latest speech as true, don't bring in the past'.

Osho was very creative in his way of talking. His talks were filled with anecdotes, jokes, harsh criticisms against many popular people, repetitive statements and sometimes pointless gossip. He gave commentaries on Upanishads, Bhagavad Gita, Buddhist texts, Zen, Sikhism, Christian mysticism, Sufism and many more. He made very clear that all these paths lead to the same goal and explained the true essence of these paths.

Osho is seen as a cult leader by many people in the world. I can understand the reason for it. The greatest bioterror attack in the United States is caused by some power hungry disciples of Osho. Even though there is no evidence that Osho was involved in it, people believe that it is not true. But Osho gave detailed explanation about everything that happened. Also, Osho was famous for owning ninety six Rolls Royces. Osho said that it was a joke. Here is what he said about them:

> *"People are very much interested in your Rolls Royces. What do You want to prove with this, so many cars and so much luxury around You?*
>
> *Why are people concerned? Then certainly they need it; then more Rolls Royces will be here. Until they stop asking me, more and more Rolls Royces are going to be here. Now it has to be seen that it is a challenge: the day nobody asks me about Rolls Royces, they will not be coming.*

People's interest in Rolls Royces shows their mind. They are not interested what is happening here. They don't ask about meditation, they don't ask about sannyas, they don't ask about people's life, love, the laughter that happens in this desert. They only ask about Rolls Royces. That means I have touched some painful nerve. And I will go on pressing it till they stop asking.

I am not a worshipper of poverty. That's what those Rolls Royces prove. I respect wealth. Nobody before me had the guts to say it. The pope cannot say that he respects wealth, although he is the wealthiest man on the earth.

I am not a hypocrite. I am the poorest man on the earth. I don't have a single cent with me. But I want to show these people what attracts their mind.

If there were no Rolls Royces here, perhaps there would be nothing for the whole world ask about me, about you, about meditation, about initiation into sannyas, about love, about anything.

It is for those idiots that I am keeping all those Rolls Royces, because they cannot move their eyes away from those Rolls Royces. And meanwhile I will go on pouring other things in their minds. Without those Rolls Royces they would not have asked a single question.

Those Rolls Royces are doing their work. Every idiot around the world is interested in them. And I want them to be somehow interested—in anything in Rajneeshpuram. Then we will manage about other things.

So tell those people—when anybody asks, tell them that "These Rolls Royces are for you idiots. Otherwise you are not interested in anything." Once they stop asking about Rolls Royces, then I will have to think of something else, whether to have rockets which are going to the moon.... I will have to think of something else.

- *The Last Testament, Osho*

Anyway, whatever Osho's intention was, nobody can say. But he was very honest, courageous and open about what he was doing. I have gone through all the negative criticisms about him and have gone through both sides of the story. Even if he was really exploiting people, it doesn't make any difference to the fact that his books and talks were tremendously helpful for me. He also played a major role in creating a worldwide awareness about human liberation. Except what I have heard and read, I can't really say what exactly happened in his life; I was not there as a witness! May be he was a fraud, may be he wasn't; but his guidance saved my life and helped me to find my own way.

Witnessing – Phase 1

As soon as I started reading Osho, I had also begun to put his witnessing meditation into practice. His witnessing meditation is an age old technique which is called Sakshi Bhav in Vedanta, Shikantaza in Zen and Sati (Mindfulness) in Buddhism. In the recent years, science has found substantial evidence for the role of mindfulness meditation in decreasing stress and increasing well being.

Soon, I went to my native place for my semester holidays and I got enough solitude to practice witnessing. A month earlier, I was practicing his other meditations like dynamic meditation, gibberish meditation and more. I created my own therapy based on his various meditation techniques and I do believe that it resolved a lot of unconscious issues.

As I progressed in my witnessing meditation, I started feeling calmer and peaceful. The thought process gradually slowed down. I continued to do it every day with great involvement. One day, when I was staring at the ceiling witnessing my thoughts, there was a brief moment of stillness with no thoughts. There was an absolute clarity and peace of mind that I had never encountered before. For the first time, I realized that I could exist without thoughts. It gave me a clear and firm knowledge that thoughts were not me.

This was like a Eureka moment. An immediate excitement followed that gave me a new strength and peace which continued for the next six months. I went back to college for the final semester, which was the happiest period that I had in the entire three years. This momentary realization was a confirmation that there was something indestructible. I interpreted it as a glimpse of my essential nature. Osho used to call this Satori.

After this, I was able to concentrate on a single task for hours and be immersed in it. As I began to learn psychology, I realized that there is a name for this. It is called 'flow'. Flow is the mental state of operation in which a person performing an activity is fully immersed in a feeling of energized focus, full involvement, and enjoyment in the process of the activity. In essence, flow is characterized by complete absorption in what one does. These states were very common and occurring everyday when I was immersed in a task. During those states, there was no feeling of my individual existence. It was as if I had disappeared.. There was just pure awareness, focus and a sense of being alive.

I felt that the complete flowering of enlightenment was very near. But I also remembered Osho saying, "there will be many beautiful moments that you would pass through. Don't make any of those moments your home. Just keep going. You may feel that you have arrived but it is not necessarily so."

I talked to one of my close friends regarding this and I started to explain to him about the beauty of meditation. I read excerpts from the books of Osho to him everyday and he was pretty impressed with a lot of Osho's revolutionary ideas. I also told him about the changes that I went through and that I felt like I might be liberated soon. But I was wrong. After about six months, the initial excitement of this Eureka moment faded. But the feeling that there was something indestructible and the everyday occurrence of flow continued and never stopped.

As I continued to read Osho's books, I felt very unfortunate that there was no enlightened master like Osho at present time that I could meet and ask my questions. I felt that if there was someone like him around, then he could guide me on my spiritual path.

Encounter the enlightened – The First Satsang With Sadhguru Jaggi Vasudev

In January 2003, I saw a wall post regarding a satsang at Marina beach, Chennai. It was titled 'Encounter the enlightened' in Tamil with the photograph of a man with a long beard. He looked like Osho. I saw the name 'Sadhguru Jaggi Vasudev' printed in the wall post. It was to be held on January 22, 2003. As soon as I saw it, I made up my mind to go there.

It was a beautiful evening at Marina beach, Chennai with thousands of people gathered. Sadhguru spoke about many things which were similar to what Osho has said about enlightenment. He spoke in a slightly different slang of Tamil flavored with Kannada accent, sounding like the slang of Tamil actor Rajinikanth. Most of his views were matching with the views of Osho. When he gave us instructions for a guided meditation, he asked everyone to focus in the middle of one's eyebrows. I remember him saying 'Just keep a slight focus in between your eyebrows, but don't concentrate'. This instantly reminded me of Osho. 'So, there is someone here who is enlightened', I told myself. But it seemed almost impossible to approach him as he was already quite popular.

He spoke about his foundation called Isha Foundation based in Coimbatore which conducts Yoga programs all over the state. At the end of the satsang, his book 'Encounter the enlightened' in Tamil was on sale. But I had no money to buy it. I returned home with mixed feelings; A happiness on having seen another modern day enlightened Guru (which I thought he was) and a disappointment for not being able to buy that book.

After finishing my course in Polytechnic, I noticed a weekly article in *Ananda Vikatan* (a Tamil magazine) authored by Sadhguru, with a title in Tamil that translates to 'Desire for everything!'.. This again reminded me of Osho's advice saying that we should not repress our desires. At the same time, another clean shaved guy with the name Nithyananda showed up with his own article in Kumudham which introduced him as another enlightened modern day Guru! But for some reason, he didn't quite appear enlightened to me, may be because he didn't have any beard. But he was caught in a scandal a few years later. That was a big story.

(Note: Recently, when I carefully noticed Sadhguru Jaggi Vasudev's talks and books, I found out that he is simply repeating Osho, including the anecdotes told by Osho, factual errors made by Osho and even the terminology used by Osho. He does all this without mentioning his name. But he claimed that he didn't read any spiritual books. He also said that everything he knew came as a mystical transmission when his guru touched him with a walking stick. During those days, I couldn't notice the lack of depth in his speech and some of his misleading descriptions of enlightenment. Because, my own thinking was completely biased. But years later after my transformation, I noticed that there is a pretension behind what he does and what he speaks. I have also noticed cultish behaviour in his followers.)

My Career in BPO and My First Isha Yoga program

After spending a few months at home reading books by Osho and searching for a job, I started working. After working in two different companies in various profiles, I finally got a job with good salary in a call center in Chennai. I started earning money, made new friendships, faced a lot of ups and downs and changed four different companies in about 5 years time. I had stopped reading spiritual books and went ahead with life. But the experience of flow happened everyday as usual. One day, I saw an announcement for Isha Yoga program which was to be conducted in Anna University for two weeks. (or one week, I don't remember). I enrolled in the program with my friend.

I had a good time over the whole program. We were given detailed information about Isha and its activities for social welfare. I also came to know more about Dhyanalinga, which is said to give you the same effect that you will get in the presence of an enlightened guru. They said that if one sat in front of Dhyanalinga and closed his eyes, he would automatically become meditative.

According to Sadhguru, the Dhyanalinga has all the seven chakras that a human being has. It has been consecrated in such a way that the energy and peace that radiates from Dhyanalinga is the same as the energy and peace radiated in the presence of someone who is enlightened. We were taught a kriya called shambhavi mahamudra, which had to be practiced twice a day. At the end of the Isha Yoga program, I immediately enrolled for the upcoming next level program called Bhava Spandana. It was a three day residential program in Isha Yoga centre, Coimbatore.

I arrived in Isha Yoga centre in the evening on the first day of Bhava Spandana. We were asked to submit our mobile phones, bags and money as there would not be any contact with the outside world for three days. I went to the dome of Dhyanalinga for the first time and meditated for fifteen minutes. To be honest, I just felt a normal relaxed state and stillness and nothing much in the presence of Dhyanalinga. The atmosphere was definitely conducive for meditation but I felt nothing more than how I would usually feel when I meditated in my home or room. I thought 'may be I am not

receptive enough or maybe the effects of the linga are overrated'…
But usually, according to Sadhguru and Osho, trying to figure out such things with our rational mind is not going to work. Their usual argument is, our logic cannot figure out something that is beyond logic. But I had an immense trust on Sadhguru Jaggi Vasudev at that time. So, I was confident that I was on the right way. (Be careful when someone discourages logical thinking though. Only the absolute reality is incomprehensible by logical thinking. But the effects that you can feel after meditation, which falls under relative reality, is something that you feel or experience. If you don't feel anything, there is always a possibility to provide a logical explanation)

I felt very insecure on the first night of Bhava Spandana. I felt like I had been disconnected from the outside world. But the next morning, the insecurity went away. I participated in all the meditations in BSP with 100% intensity. Some of the meditations involved action and were similar to the concept of dynamic meditation by Osho. The feelings of oneness and peace I felt there was not new to me since I had already experienced that with my witnessing meditation. But the three days were very beautiful and the overall experience was good.

After the BSP program, I came back to Chennai and my regular routine started again. A lot of things happened in my life then which gave me extreme suffering. I used to become emotionally dependent on certain people that I liked a lot; If the people I liked didn't give me the same attention to me, it made me to suffer and become anxious. That was exactly what was happening in those days. It took a few months for me to become alright again.

Exploring Spirituality Further

I had bought two books by Sadhguru, 'Encounter the enlightened' and 'Mystic's musings'. The book Mystic's Musings was about many things that any rational person would never want to believe in. But I had no problem with that because of the trust I had in Sadhguru. I always remembered what Sadhguru said, 'Don't believe me or disbelieve me! Don't come to a conclusion about anything by yourself. Be ready to say I don't know and be a seeker'… Osho has said the same thing many times. It has always been my own approach to life too. I finished reading those two books and watched a lot of videos of Sadhguru's talks.

I continued my witnessing meditation and I had many peak experiences. Peak experiences were described by psychologist Abraham Maslow as "rare, exciting, oceanic, deeply moving, exhilarating, elevating experiences that generate an advanced form of perceiving reality, and are even mystic and magical in their effect upon the experimenter". In the meantime, I read the teachings of Ramana Maharshi. I also came to know about Eckhart tolle and his awakening experience. I read three of his books, 'The Power of now', 'A New Earth' and 'The Stillness speaks'.

The Truth About Spiritual Enlightenment

I came across the teachings of another Indian guru named Poonjaji. Soon I discovered that there are many people who claim to be enlightened, especially in the west. Some of them I read about were Gangaji, Andrew Cohen, Ramesh Balsekar, Mooji, Joan Tollifson etc. I read their testimonies about the awakening experiences. Are each of one of them really enlightened or they just had some peak experiences and glimpses of the reality? There seemed to be no way to find out. Can we really draw a single line called 'Enlightenment' in someone's life which is the ultimate line after which there is no progress further? (Later I came to understand that enlightenment is just a beginning and it goes deeper and deeper as the time goes by). Is everyone who claims to be enlightened talk about that same line? I emailed a couple of these people and got answers too. They said that their enlightenment was a gradual process and not something that occurred in the single moment as Osho described. They also didn't have a totally thoughtless mind, ability to leave the body at will or memories of previous incarnation. Did Osho exaggerate the effects of enlightenment by saying that there would be no thoughts or did these people just conclude that they were enlightened with no basis to support their claim? I had no answers to these questions.

I had already integrated Karma Yoga, Jnana Yoga and Bhakti yoga in my life and made my life itself a spiritual practice. Every moment was an opportunity for me to explore the depths of my own unconsciousness and clear out the clouds which were hiding my own reality. The concepts of Advaita taught me 'acceptance'. I learnt to accept the life as it is.

My Marriage and the Life After

I got married in December 2008. The first two years of my marriage were spent in a lot of conflicts and quarrels between me and my wife. I became addicted to alcohol and started drinking twice or thrice a week. I started learning about PHP programming, chess tactics, astronomy, photoshop and many other things. Photography became my new hobby. Nothing much happened in my life those days. I used to go to Ramana Maharishi's ashram in Tiruvannamalai with my wife whenever I got a chance and spend time in meditation.

Two years later, I moved to my hometown Tirunelveli and got a job there. I spent my time in learning, writing articles and trying out new things on the internet. New interests always popped up and got me going. The moments of flow helped me to stay on focus.

After another two years, I moved to Coimbatore. I started exploring places nearby. I climbed mountains and hills on weekends and took pictures. I enjoyed trekking in various places of Nilgiris. I had stopped drinking alcohol and started experimenting with cannabis. It seemed to be a magic herb. It enhanced my creativity, focus and compassion. We had no kids and there were no big responsibilities. I used to visit Isha Yoga centre occasionally but wasn't thinking much about enlightenment or spirituality. I didn't think anything about the future or the past. Living in the present moment was quite satisfying but there was still something incomplete in me which was yearning for fulfillment.

On May 5, 2014, I climbed the Velliangiri mountains. It is a holy mountain near Coimbatore. Isha Yoga centre is right at the foot of the mountains. Sadhguru had said that he himself had spent time there and he had said that many enlightened people left their bodies there and their energy can be still felt in the mountains. There was no one to accompany me to trek the mountain so I went all by myself. I started walking uphills at about 7:30 AM and reached the summit by 1:30 PM. The mountain is very steep and difficult to climb. The view from the top is amazing. I had the darshan of the linga in the summit, took rest for about 30 minutes and started walking downhill. I took many photographs and finally reached the bottom at about 7:30 PM. The experience was wonderful.

The Life Changing Transformation

The trip to Velliangiri mountains triggered the seeker in me and I decided to go deep in meditation as much as I could. I started paying attention to every moment, every thought and every sensation. I made very clear to me that whatever I observe, perceive, think, experience and know is not me. I witnessed all the passing emotions and moods as a passive observer.

I went to Isha yoga centre every week, took bath in Theerthakund and meditated for an hour. I spent almost half of the day there. In the office, my nature of job was to talk to the customers over the phone during the whole night and answer their questions. I became deeply involved in the present moment and enjoyed my work. I soon stopped thinking about many things in the external world. I noticed my thoughts slowing down leaving a peaceful, clear stillness in the large gaps between each thought. Very soon, I started feeling intense euphoria at times which lasted for hours. The quality of my work increased, the clarity in my voice and speech increased and I started to feel waves of bliss in my head. It was like a cool breeze flowing in my head.

Soon, I stopped my interactions with other people. It was not my conscious decision but happened automatically. I couldn't believe that all these things were happening to me. I didn't feel any intense negative emotion or anxiety but almost the whole day at my work was filled with bliss and peace. Soon, the psychological boundaries between me and the world started to disappear. I started getting a lot of attention and I was pretty sure that something tremendous was happening.

I went to attend Sadhguru's darshan (a discourse session) that happened in the Isha ashram on June 18th and 19th, 2014. I felt one with the whole universe during the entire discourse. The feeling of oneness with the world was then continuous. Whatever I did seemed to happen without much of my conscious will. Everything I did was spontaneous like a river flowing down the hills. The doer in me seemed to have completely disappeared and everything seemed to be happening out of cosmic will instead of my own will.

It was a huge blessing. Every day at work, I felt tremendously happy and satisfied. For the first time in my life, I felt complete and fulfilled. I wondered, 'Is it really possible for me to suffer ever again?'... I felt like the king of the whole world.

I went to another satsang that was held on July 12, 2014 (Guru Purnima day). I remember getting on the bus feeling so light as if I had no weight on the body. Everything seemed to be so transparent. During the entire satsang, I was immersed in my Self. That night while I was lying on my bed, there was a sudden clarity. It seemed that my search was over. There was nothing else to achieve and nothing more to do to make me complete.

The Days After the Transformation

The excitement and the wave of bliss were gradually reduced in the days to come. Though I no longer felt the waves and breeze of bliss in my head, being peaceful and complete has been the normal state of my mind from those days of transformation to till date.

Though I had no doubt that the journey as a human being in my life was over and it wouldn't matter if I die at any moment, the transformation didn't exactly fit into the description of enlightenment as implied by Osho and Sadhguru Jaggi Vasudev. When I thought about it later after the next two years, I noted down my observation of the changes it had made in my thinking, well being and my way of life:

- Self image is no longer important to me.
- My past no longer plays a role in giving me a mental identity in my mind.
- I cannot think about future the same way I did before. In a sense, I seemed to have lost the sense of time. I don't and can't rely on an event in the future for satisfaction.
- I stopped feeling that there is an 'other'. The psychological boundaries between me and the world disappeared. A lot of concepts in Psychology doesn't seem to apply to me or relevant to me. For example, I no longer felt the psychological self-consciousness and cognitive dissonance.
- Emotions like sadness and fear seems to have disappeared. In fact, fear was the first thing to disappear. But I continue to show the sign of a sudden fear in my facial expression and bodily movements like knee jerk reactions when there is something that sudden and is physically threatening. (For example, if a moving vehicle suddenly comes close to me enough to hit me, I respond to it in the usual way. But it doesn't have the same impact on my mind as it did before. May be it is so subtle but I don't usually feel fear or sadness)
- I continue to feel angry when I am disturbed by others. As a person, I always used to be high in neuroticism and easily

angered ever since I was a child. It seemed to a genetic factor. It makes sense to assume that meditation or an awakening experience doesn't mysteriously change a person's genetics. But the factors that will make me angry were reduced completely. I could easily change my mood from being angry to being normal.

- It is not like feeling continuous bliss and being drugged all the time. But there is always a peace and fulfillment and there is no longer a feeling that something is incomplete.

- The thoughts have not completely disappeared but they have been tremendously reduced. My thinking is usually not about the past or the present. For example, at any moment I may be thinking 'May be there is life on one of the moons on Saturn', or 'How come hummingbirds are really too small? They are cute'… I hardly think about me.

- There is absolutely nothing paranormal. I don't have any memories of past life and have never seen a damn aura in my life.

- Biological drives like food and sex motivates my behavior as usual. But motivation theories like expectancy theory or goal setting theory doesn't seem to apply for me much. I am not driven to do something because I will get something as a result in three months time. I have to remember to consciously involve myself to do it. But I will do something to get a bottle of brandy to drink this evening. These days I have developed a conscious practice of planning ahead and thinking about doing things which are necessary for the future. The drawback with that is, I may completely forget to do it.

Also, while some changes obviously occurred as an immediate result of the transformation, some changes are gradual and still occurring within me. It took a long time to learn to live with this transformed personality and there were challenges that I faced. It is hard to put it in language, because in one way or the other, it will be misleading.

I continue to learn by my experience with this new phenomenon (in fact, people will say that it is not a new thing, it is just a person's real essence which was and will be always present. That is true... But it is still gives a new outlook. The way it affects our behavior and our experiences is new).'

But there are other concepts which are associated with enlightenment and mentioned by many of the enlightenment gurus we have seen so far... Here is a list of some of those concepts:

- Being enlightened is like being in ecstatic bliss 24/7.
- Once you are enlightened, you will remember your past lives.
- You radiate some kind of energy which can be felt by people near you.
- You can recognize another enlightened person by sight.
- You don't have any cravings or ego anymore... You are just pure consciousness with no thoughts, no cravings, and no ego!

- If you want to die, you can do it by your own will and by causing no pain or damage to the body.
- You can see auras of other people.

Nothing like that ever happened to me after the transformation so far. But some people used to say that I was the happiest person in the world. I had a smile in my face whenever I met any of my friends and I looked happy and full of energy all the time. But I did face challenges and even went through some emotional pain from time to time. They were not at all felt personal and left no trace in my psyche but they did give me a hard time.

Another thing that is noteworthy is that I felt like I was born again. This is consistent with the concept of 'dvija' in Indian tradition. In a couple of months after transformation, I was left with no motivation. I felt like there is nothing more to do with this life. So, I had to create a motivation that would give me a direction for life. For the time being, I decided to perform as effectively as I could, at work.

But I noticed that when it came to social behaviour, I made no attempt to impress others, influence the behaviour of others or even gossip with others, which affected a few things in my life. I was running a family. So, it was very important for my dependants that I influence other people to get things to happen the way I wanted them to happen. For example, I needed to get promoted soon so that I could take care of my family in a better way. Because of these demands, certain things began to change. I had to consciously create a subtle ego and personality. I also had to choose a mission for my life, (not a goal that I want to reach but a direction I want to go towards) which will keep me motivated to do things in life. These changes happened very gradually and soon I realized that I had been relearning certain things in life as a total new born. My brain was creating fresh associations with each stimuli and experience. But all of this happened very consciously and I could see those changes for what they were. I also noticed that my genetic factors were intact and they still influenced the way I thought and behaved.

Around May 2016, I bought a book called 'Psychology' 5th edition written by Robert A. Baron and Girishwar Mishra. Learning psychology changed a lot of things. It was very interesting to learn about why people behaved the way they did and it offered a lot of new insights to my own transformation. (I was also using cannabis everyday during this time). At the same time, I also suffered from Insomnia because I always felt energetic and I could never get myself to sleep so easily. Sleep deprivation, vigorous study of psychology and hard work at office caused me to be active all the time. My highest record was set when I was awake continuously for 45 hours with maximum activity.

I started seeing many connections in totally disconnected happenings of my life in the past. Things were happening so fast that I was not able to keep myself balanced. It was like riding in a roller coaster most of the time. Every bit of my body and mind was throbbing with energy. The valence of my emotions kept changing every hour.

It would be miserable for an hour; then I would feel peaceful as if nothing had happened, for the next hour.

I started behaving like a lunatic and things got worse. Soon I left my job and went to my parent's home. The roller coaster continued and I was admitted in a psychiatric hospital for 10 days. The doctor prescribed haloperidol and chlorpromazine. (They are usually prescribed for schizophrenia. But I know the symptoms and I was not schizophrenic.) The doctors didn't even bother to talk to me or counsel me. And, there was a serious side effect with these tablets; they cause Akathisia, the worst disorder one could ever get. If you have akathisia you cannot sit still or stand in one place for more than 3-4 minutes. You will always have an urge to keep moving your body. I suffered from akathisia for more than a month. It was cured by taking trihexyphenidyl and clonazepam (The doctors were not helpful. I had to search in Wikipedia to find out which antipsychotic drugs were causing the problem and just skip them).

These symptoms that I underwent is actually a spiritual crisis that I described earlier. They are supposed to be diagnosed and treated differently. But usually, a lot of psychiatrists who are not aware of this treat these symptoms as indications of a regular mental disorder. There is an integration period after the transformation (the transformation that breaks the duality). During this integration period, there may be a lot of difficulties which are usually not discussed in spiritual books.

Now, I feel like I have become a grown up boy in this new second birth. (I am talking about 'dvija'; not about a previous incarnation). I have a better clarity of what exactly happened in me in the last three and a half years. U.G Krishnamurti went through a similar transformation in his life and he used to call it a 'calamity'. Also, he has said in his interviews that he had to learn certain things from scratch as well. I haven't read his books much, but the word 'calamity' actually suits what I went through.

After I was cured from Akathisia, I settled down in my new job and everything became fine. Life is beautiful now. As far as my subjective well-being is concerned, there is no way it can be any better than this. I am not seeking anything anymore (as I already feel complete and liberated) but I am still interested in this concept of enlightenment and find out the neural correlates of it in the brain. I cannot do this alone. But my mission is to contribute towards a scientific research on human transformation. I spend my time reading psychology journals, science papers and articles, writing blog posts, reading about the awakening experiences of others etc. I maintain a blog http://nellaishanmugam.wordpress.com.

My life is now full of awe and curiosity, and this awakening seems to be deepening; I see no limits for the depth. Whether this is enlightenment or not doesn't matter to me. If someone says that this is enlightenment, I would probably say 'oh, I see'... If they say I still have to work towards another shift called 'enlightenment', I wouldn't bother about it. Because, anything beyond this will be an unnecessary luxury. But the bottom line is, it put an end to a life in which I considered myself as a person separate from the existence. Now, there is always a feeling of boundlessness, satisfaction and peace which leaves no room for further seeking. There is nothing to seek anymore and there is no feeling of dissatisfaction, worry, anxiety, depression or insecurity anymore.. My way of living is totally different from the way the others around me live their lives. It is indeed a blessing! It feels as if a huge load has been taken off of my shoulders.

The path to liberation is very unique to each individual in a way. Because everyone has a different type of genetic makeup and upbringing. Everyone has to find his own path. But the concepts presented in this book should give anyone a starting point and should guide you to find your own path and follow your own light.

Chapter Twelve: Be A Light Unto Yourself

It is said that Buddha's final message was 'Be a light unto yourself'. He said this on his last day on the earth. Ananda, Buddha's closest disciple and cousin was weeping and worried about his spiritual progress. He said to Buddha, 'What am I going to do after your death? Who will help me with my spiritual path? Who will guide me to attain Nirvana? You came to this earth as a light, to remove the darkness of this world. Who will be our light after you are gone?". Buddha said, ""Appo Deepo Bhava". It means 'be a light unto yourself'. It is also translated as 'Be an island to yourself'. But the meaning is the same.

The true Guru is within you. Your own inner light is pretty capable of guiding you towards liberation. Even though every human being seems to be in the pursuit of different things in the world, everyone are really searching for liberation. You may not know it or recognize it. But deep down in your heart, there is a longing to get liberated. Once you recognize this longing and once you get the basic idea about the spiritual path, your own light is capable of taking you there. Remember, I am using the words very casually.. Liberation is not out there, there is really no journey and nowhere to go.

But more than any other time in the history, the message 'Be a light unto yourself' needs to be conveyed to the spiritual seekers of today's time. Because, 99% of what is happening in the name of spirituality is fake. Spirituality has become one of the most profitable businesses in the world. Spiritual organizations often come off as brainwashing cults.

Modern gurus don't and can't interact with millions of their so called disciples because they are very far away from the reach of these common people. But these poor disciples develop a lot of attachment towards their gurus and start a cult of personality. The disciples create an idealized, heroic, and even worshipful image of a guru, while the guru is busy flying helicopters and playing golf. I am not saying that a guru shouldn't do any of these things. A liberated person is not bound by any of his actions. But this organization based spiritual guidance becomes ultimately useless and even harmful. There is no personal interaction between the guru and the millions of his disciples at all! Instead, disciples get totally distracted from their own spiritual path and give way more importance to the unreachable guru. Because of the popular public image their Guru has, the disciples identify with their gurus and the organizations and start parroting everything their guru says.

I am not exaggerating. I have observed a lot of people who are crazy fans of a particular guru or spiritual organization but they don't have any idea what liberation is about. They indulge in verbally abusing the critics and calling other people as 'idiots' and 'stupids'. They let their intelligence get completely hijacked by their emotions. Instead of developing non-attachment, they develop attachment to their guru and his spiritual organization.

Who is Maitreya?

Recently I was thinking about Maitreya, the future Buddha of the world. It is said that Buddha promised everyone that he would reincarnate again in this planet 2500 years after his death. I don't know if this story is true or not. But I noticed that it has a great metaphorical significance. The word 'maitreya' just means 'a friend'. I don't see maitreya as an avatar or incarnation but as a replacement for a guru. The guru disciple system is not going to work anymore as it did in the olden days. There are a lot of reasons for that. First, a lot of power hungry and intelligent people are looking to take up the role of a guru because it is a great business opportunity. You can't know who is fake and who is not fake! Second, the guru is only for the namesake. He can't really offer any personal guidance because he is too far away from your reach.

A person who calls himself as a guru or sadhguru may exploit people. But a person who wants to be your spiritual friend cannot exploit you. A friend has the same status as yours. He is not any superior to you. Liberation is not a status or a post either. I was wondering if this is the real meaning for 'Maitreya'. It simply means gurus are going to be replaced by spiritual friends.

A friend will not expect a free labor from you. A friend will not ask you to surrender to him. A friend will not ask you to bow down to him. Most importantly, a friend will not ask you to call him sadhguru. He will gossip with you, smoke, drink and eat with you and will just show you the way. He will make sure that you don't follow him but follow your own light.

There is another word called 'kalyana mitra' in Buddhism which also means spiritual friend. In Upaddha Sutta, Buddha says that when a monk has admirable people as friends and companions, he can be expected to develop and pursue the noble eightfold path.

Recently, I was watching a video discourse of Osho. And I was surprised to hear Osho talking about the exact same thing:

> Buddha declared before his death that he would be coming again after twenty-five centuries, and that his name would be Maitreya. Maitreya means the friend. Buddhas don't come back; no enlightened person ever comes back, so it is just a way of saying....

> What he was saying is of tremendous importance. It has nothing to do with his coming back; he cannot come back. What he meant was that the ancient relationship between the Master and the disciple would become irrelevant in

twenty-five centuries. It was his clarity of perception -- he was not predicting anything -- just his clarity to see that as things are changing, as they have changed in the past and as they go on changing, it would take at least twenty-five centuries for the Master and disciple relationship to become out of date. Then the enlightened Master will be only the friend.

- *The Last Testament, Vol. 3, Osho*

It was either a beautiful coincidence or probably cryptomnesia! I don't recall watching this video before or reading it in a book before, but who knows? May be I read it sometime in the distant past. But this thought about maitreya crossed my mind quite a few times in the last few weeks, before I watched Osho's video. After looking at some of the ugly things which are happening in the name of spirituality and under the leadership of a guru, I became convinced that this guru-disciple system has become outdated.

Don't follow anyone!

There is another quote from Osho that I want to mention here:

"All the old religions of the world are based on that statement. But that statement is a psychological exploitation of man. I cannot say, "Come follow me."

First, those who have said it have crippled humanity, have made humanity helpless. They certainly fulfilled a certain need. People don't want to be on their own. They don't have the guts to create their own path, to walk and create it. They want to be led. But they don't know that if you are being led, slowly slowly, even if you have eyes, you will lose them. You will be seeing through the eyes of Jesus, Krishna, Mohammed. Your eyes will not be needed; in fact your eyes will cause a disturbance."

• *From Unconsciousness to Consciousness, Osho*

This is 100% true.. Even if a guru himself says 'don't follow me', people will still follow him. It is a tendency for most of the people. Sometimes such following and parroting happen so unconsciously that these disciples would not recognize it. These disciples would say 'No, I am not a blind follower of my guru. He also doesn't ask anyone to follow him!". But they don't realize that they are wrong. Their long term association with an authority figure makes them slowly and gradually to follow and parrot the authority. I have witnessed this many times.

As Osho says, one must have the courage to create his own path to walk. In fact, each person's path is unique. Since there are 7 billion people in the world, there are also 7 billion spiritual paths. Most of the time, only those who find their own path are the ones who get liberated. Each person has different upbringing, different genetic makeup and unique personality traits. Once a person develops the necessary awareness and insight about some of the simple things that we have discussed, he can manage the journey on his own.

Here is a summary of the most important points discussed in this book:

- Learning to discriminate between the subject and the object
- Understanding that the subject has no attributes at all.
- Understanding that the objects are impermanent, not self and clinging to them causes suffering.
- Observing and understanding the tendencies of your mind and your ego.
- Practicing open monitoring, focused and dynamic meditations as much as necessary.
- Practicing and developing witnessing, integrating it into everyday activities and gradually making it into a 24/7 process.

The above points cover the core of spirituality. I can confidently say that if you understand and implement the above mentioned points, that should be sufficient. You don't have to know anything more than this. The core wisdom of ancient spiritual traditions has been summarized in these points.

I would also recommend reading this book again and again to get a better understanding. Remember, liberation is about you and you only. There is no need to be a follower, a disciple, a devotee or a volunteer! Your inner light is your guru.. You can also take this whole existence as your guru. You can have as many spiritual friends as you want. Remember to always follow your own light!

Made in the USA
Las Vegas, NV
29 July 2021

27243959R00129